Tom,

Thanks again for supporting the book. Hope you enjoy the stories.

Rich

THE GUIDES

A COLLECTION OF UNTAMED STORIES

RIDR KNOWLTON

ISBN: 978-1-954614-12-3 Hard Cover
ISBN: 978-1-954614-13-0 Soft Cover

Edited by: Monika Dziamka
A portion of proceeds from this book will be donated to charity.

Published by Warren Publishing
Charlotte, NC
www.warrenpublishing.net
Printed in the United States

Illustrations credit: Martha Knowlton
Cover photo credit: Ridr Knowlton

Pack train stream crossing in the Brooks Range, Alaska. Moments after this photo was taken, I went flying down the embankment on my own horse, hanging on for dear life.

The Guides *is dedicated to my friend, Bill Fuchs, a real adventurer, tough as nails, and one of the most interesting people I have ever met.*

ACKNOWLEDGMENTS

I would like to thank all those with whom I have shared a campfire, tent, tarp, deer stand, stream, flats boat, drift boat, center console, truck cab, garage, taxidermy studio, rocky outcrop, tree line, horse trail, mule-drawn wagon, covey, base camp, spike camp, swamp, logging road, dove field, and duck blind. I have learned from all of you.

In particular, I would like to thank:

- My dad, Dick Knowlton, a turkey hunter, permit fly fisherman, and the most hardcore sportsman I know, for introducing me to the outdoors and sporting world.
- My mom, Martha Knowlton, a well-read artist, for showing me the subtle beauty of the outdoors and for correcting my poor grammar.
- Mike Owens, a professor of hunting, for teaching me to become a selective hunter.
- John Heagy, a mentor, sporting gentleman, and master of the Dutch oven, for opening doors to adventure and for inspiring me to climb mountains.
- Jimmy Ewing, for his writing inspiration and for expounding the outdoors with talent and humor.

- Blane Woodfin, Hammy, Dick, Coll, Tom, Sam, J.B., Maddox, Brad White, and all my fly fishing, bird hunting, and climbing buddies from Atlanta, for years of great stories, adventures, and laughter around campfires.
- Chap Esterhuizen, Rob Lurie, Roy Aylward and the mystically skilled native trackers and scouts I have been lucky to follow in the African bush.
- And a very special thank you to Mark and Valerie Condict, Bill and Linda Fuchs, Seth Vernon, Rob Pasfield, and Mike McCann, for so many enjoyable times together and trusting me with your stories.
- Finally, and most importantly, thank you to my wife Sue and our two amazing kids, each accomplished sportspeople in their own right, for supporting and joining my passion for the outdoors, invaluable editing, and allowing so many antlers to hang on our walls.

Contents

FOREWORD   1

AN EARLY CONNECTION   15

BIG FISH   27

COASTAL GUIDE   39

THE CONDICTS OF WYOMING   46

MOUNTAIN GUIDES   74

THE FUCHS   94

  - The Everglades   95

  - The Jungle   101

  - Africa   114

SNAKES   128

EPILOGUE   146

BIBLIOGRAPHY   148

ENDNOTES   150

FOREWORD

My guide was an Inuit tracker. We were on the western boarder of Nunavut in far northern Canada, just below the Arctic Circle. We had spent the morning observing caribou that were supposed to be migrating farther south, through Canada's Northwest Territories. It was already September in the arctic, but the migration was delayed that year (2009) and the herds were still up north. We had taken three good bulls and did not need more meat for camp. The rest of the day would be spent leaning against our packs on the tundra ground, watching the slow migration, and listening to my guide relate incredible stories.

A few days prior, our small group of hunters learned of the delayed migration and called a last-minute audible in Yellowknife, an old gold-mining town and the capital of the Northwest Territories. Along with our outfitter, we decided to fly farther north via floatplane into Nunavut in an effort to find the herds. Nunavut is the largest territory in Canada and the farthest north. It encompasses much of the Canadian arctic and is mostly accessed by plane or boat.

I had invited my father to join me on the trip. I was forty-one years old, and my dad was in his mid-sixties. We were joined by three other hunters, all from the US. Our bush pilot agreed with the plan to fly us to the more northern location, and our outfitter secured necessary permits to hunt the new territory. The floatplane was packed tight with gear and two or three hunters. Any gear or hunters who did not make the weight cutoff would have to wait for a return flight later in the day, if weather permitted. A few years earlier, in a similar situation in western Alaska, I had opted to let the gear and other hunters go first, and it turned into a long wait. This time, I made the cut, squeezing myself and my gear into a jump seat in the rear of the plane on the first flight.

The flight from Yellowknife into Nunavut follows a northeast route, taking off from the dark waters of Great Slave Lake, over small inlets littered with toy houses perched on bare rock islands, and north across the vast boreal forest as it transitions to tundra. As the bush plane flew north, the last tree of the Canadian forest disappeared below.

I looked for it, the northernmost tree—the last tree, before all trees disappear from view and the land below is swept into muted colors of the treeless tundra. I have read the word "tundra" actually means "treeless land." Dark indigo lakes of all sizes were scattered to the horizons. The few roads crossing the tundra fall into the lakes, pointless dead-ends without winter's frozen ice needed for the brave truckers to cross the bodies of water, bridging a connection to the road re-emerging on the far bank. The roads service big diamond mines, and one appeared below the plane like a small, confined city. The mine seemed too remote to be logistically possible, like the oil refineries in the Mississippi Delta. I strained my neck as we flew over the mine, fascinated with the contained activity below, and imagining life there during the long, dark winter.

We continued northeast and crossed into Nunavut territory. Our bush pilot located camp and circled a few times to determine the best direction for landing on the neighboring lake. The twin pontoons nestled into the water as we landed, and the pilot powered the small plane right up to the gravel beach below camp. I stepped out on wobbly legs and got my bearings.

Our hosts were an Inuit family. The patriarch, who would guide my dad and me, was a seasoned tracker and guide. Over the course of the hunt, the two of us built a mutual trust, and he opened up about life in the arctic and the deep spiritual connection he felt to his remote home. To maintain that trust, I have kept his real name out of this book.

Joining him at the camp were his wife and niece, who ran the camp, cooked meals, and dried caribou fat on handmade racks by the water. His nephew was there to help guide, along with an American biologist, who guided caribou hunts during the summer months and conducted wildlife research during the winters.

We gathered our gear, walked up the gravel path from the rocky beach, and investigated camp, an abandoned arctic research station laid out on a slight rise above the lake where our plane landed. The main building was large enough to house minimal cooking equipment and a few tables. Three or four tent-sized wooden structures and an outhouse lined a path following the water's edge. Our "cabin" had two cots and a small gas heater. The walls were painted white and decorated with dozens of nails sticking out to hang or dry gear. We quickly learned the gas heater worked too well in the tiny space and pondered the proper balance between cracking open the hinged wooden door for fresh, cold air, and maintaining a slight protective barrier from roaming grizzly. The interior arctic grizzly bear, which was not uncommon in the area, is a fraction of the size of its coastal brown bear cousins, but can be far more aggressive; protein is sparse on the tundra. We elected to crack open the door, litter the doorway with everything we had that would make noise if stepped on by a bear, and sleep with loaded rifles leaning next to our cots.

The very next day, we found the migration, and over the following week, we took world-class Central Canada barren ground caribou that, to this day, rank respectfully among the all-time hunting records of Boone and Crockett. Looking back on that incredible hunting trip, what strikes me is that my clearest and fondest memories are not of the successful hunting, which was superior. Instead, I think about the sights and smells of the tundra and camp, the wildlife, the fascinating people we met—and their stories.

The far north is a mystical place. Small stacks of stone called "inuksuk" stood sentinel over the tundra in all directions from our camp, left tens or maybe hundreds of years before by Inuit hunters for navigation purposes or to mark caribou paths. Some, called "inunnguaq," are shaped like ancient people. I remember how I stared from our outboard boat at one particular inunnguaq, which stood on a small hill, for twenty minutes, convinced I was looking at one of our hunting party who had gotten lost from camp. As we passed the humanoid silhouette, I could see the individual stones, stacked perfectly in the form of a person standing with their arms outstretched, bound together by nothing but gravity and placement of the rocks. I remember, too, how the arctic skies were lit pastel much of the day and glowed with neon green aurora at night. Upon closer inspection, the land was surprisingly colorful: lichen blooms covered rocks with cherry red, lemon yellow, deep purple, black, and white. Over time, you learn to pick your path across the tundra by avoiding the colors that gravitate toward softer ground. I preferred to follow the white lichen, which grew on firmer, rocky surfaces.

From a distance, tundra colors all blend into a reddish hue. The tundra is sparse, with only the slightest rolling terrain. The caribou come in waves. You will see nothing for hours, or possibly days. Then one lone caribou will appear. I remember the first one I saw. It was a great bull, and I took dozens of pictures, not realizing hundreds of caribou would soon pour over the same hill moments later. After we would take a caribou, we kept vigilant watch for bear while we cleaned the animal. Nothing was wasted. The meat and fat was dried, the hide was stripped, the string-like sinew was stored for later use, and the brains were stored as a delicacy. We butchered the caribou right on the soft ground. The animal would get quartered so we could efficiently carry the meat back to our small aluminum LUND outboard boat, which we used to navigate the tundra via the endless lakes. The fat was cut out in thin layers and immediately laid over rocks to begin drying as we cleaned the rest of the caribou. The slick, white fat shined on the dark rocks, luminescent beacons to every bear for miles. We ate caribou every day.

Early on the first day of hunting, we took our outboard far north from camp. We found a slight rise in the tundra, beached the boat, hiked a low hill, and decided to sit and glass for caribou from our vantage. By "glass," I mean to look for game through binoculars or scopes. Even large animals are easily invisible to the naked eye in their natural habitat, and hunters spend long hours, or even days, "glassing" for signs of life in the wild. As we quietly sat and glassed, a black arctic fox suddenly appeared just yards away. The fox watched us with spooky light eyes. He would be pure white in a few months but was perfectly camouflaged in his dark coat for September. He disappeared after a few minutes. My dad and I glanced at each other and smiled. From time to time in the wild, during a hunting or fishing trip, we come across an animal we like to believe is a spirit of my grandfather checking in on us. In the past, we've had such moments with ravens, wild boar, and even a snow-white gyrfalcon in Alaska. This time it was a pitch-black fox.

Distant movement, probably a mile away, caught our eyes. Sure enough, two white dots were crossing a far hill. It took us a moment to realize it was two pure-white arctic wolves chasing a female caribou that had been separated from the herd. We watched the wolves run the caribou for over twenty minutes before all three disappeared over the hill. It was a highlight of the trip for me. We saw wolf tracks every day but never saw the white wolves again.

Each evening after dinner at camp, I cornered the biologist and asked him about his research and life in the arctic. "What would you eat?" I inquired early in the week. He didn't hesitate at all with the answer: "Snowy owl." They hunted and ate owl. He reminded me that in the arctic, you eat whatever protein and calories you can find.

Toward the end of the trip, I asked the biologist what experience in the arctic he would never forget. He told me about one foggy night when he had lost his bearing from camp. As he tried to retrace his steps in the dark, he suddenly realized he was not alone. He began to see large shadows around him. He had walked right into a herd of musk ox. A musk ox is a large prehistoric-looking beast with long, shaggy hair that resembles a wooly yak. They live in the far reaches of the arctic in some of the harshest conditions on earth. "I was scared," he told me. He backed away slowly, doing his best to not startle the big animals, and eventually found his way back to camp.

A delicacy of the far north is the ptarmigan, pronounced "tarmagin." Ptarmigan are grouse-sized birds that live on the tundra. They are one of the few birds that grow fur on their feet instead of feathers, protecting them from the frigid conditions. During molting, the ptarmigan will change color from a muted brown of the summer to pure snow white, a highly effective winter camouflage.

One afternoon, my guide asked if I would like to go ptarmigan hunting. Having eaten caribou for breakfast, lunch, and dinner for several days, I jumped at the opportunity. He asked if I would like to borrow a gun. I was curious how they hunted ptarmigan the traditional way. "With stones," he said.

First, you need to find your ammo, or rocks, which are plentiful. The challenge was finding the right size for accuracy and weight.

My guide selected fine stones, much like selecting a delicate 410 gauge quail gun. I picked up rocks, more akin to an eight gauge goose gun. Fortunately, unlike their southern cousins, which explode from cover when approached, ptarmigan rely on the art of camouflage as a first line of defense. Lucky for me, this allowed us to approach the ptarmigan relatively closely. The still birds then made an easy shot, or toss, for my guide. My shots, or heaves, were heavy, loud, and less efficient. My guide quickly harvested two fat birds. An hour later, I managed a lucky throw at a lazy bird willing to give itself to the cause to get me to leave, and we returned to the camp kitchen with three ptarmigan breasts, mine already tenderized.

I credit our guide for probably saving a life that week. The three of us—my dad, our guide, and myself—were motoring across a large lake in that tiny boat when we suddenly hit a submerged pile of rocks. The impact was hard enough to knock the outboard engine off the transom. Miraculously, our guide kept the boat upright after impact. He kept all of us from tipping into that frigid water, hundreds of yards from shore. If the boat had flipped, I am not sure all three of us would have been able to gather ourselves on the boat hull after hitting the freezing water. We paddled to shore, hiked to a slight rise, and found no radio signal. As the afternoon progressed, we began to resign ourselves to a long night when we noticed a thick white wall of snow crossing the lake in our direction. We didn't mind having an uncomfortable night on the rocky shore and figured our guide's nephew would eventually find us the next day, but an early-season blizzard was something entirely different.

We gathered a tarp that had been stuck under some gear in the boat and began a survival plan for the storm. As the blizzard rolled closer, it brought early darkness and all three of us began waving our flashlights on the chance his nephew might have already come out searching for us when we had not returned to camp. By nothing but pure luck, he was indeed searching the same lake and saw our lights in the darkness. He motored over, and we all piled into his small boat not ten minutes before the whiteout storm engulfed the shore. I sat low in the boat as we motored away from the storm, listening to the sound of cold lake water lapping the bow in the dark, grateful nothing had happened to my dad. Bright green northern lights spun into corkscrews overhead, and we pushed on through the night toward camp.

As the days passed, I became interested in learning more about who my guide was as a person. I found him to be at absolute peace with his life. He knew his world on the tundra was vast and mine, near a city, was small. He knew his resources were limitless and mine were controlled. I knew, at some level, he felt sorry for me. One night over caribou stew, I asked his wife how they had met. She smiled and said, "He saved my life." I dipped my bread in my piping-hot bowl and asked to hear their story.

She grew up in a closely knit Inuit community clustered in the far northern reaches of Nunavut. I asked her for more detail on the location of the village. She looked at me and said, "Where the land turns to salt water." To this day, that is the greatest description of a location I have ever heard. I later learned the village was far to the north, above the Arctic Circle, near Victoria Island.

She went on to tell me how a small group from the village had not returned as expected from a visit to a neighboring community. Their last known location was over sixty miles away, across broken ice and frozen ground. They were overdue, and a terrible blizzard was quickly engulfing the area. It was unknown whether the group would make the blind push home, or dig in and try to weather the storm. Either would likely kill them. The village's elder council was called together to decide whether or not to send a rescue party.

The council's decision had dire implications. Could the village risk the lives of their most skilled and valued trackers in an effort to save the lives of a small group? Weather conditions were quickly worsening, increasing the likelihood the rescuers themselves would also become lost and die in the storm. Visibility would be non-existent. Temperatures would drop to sixty degrees below zero, and winds would blow at hurricane force. Tools and machinery would freeze instantly.

The council voted against a rescue. It was too risky, and the trackers were too valuable to the survival of the overall village. The lost villagers would have to fend for themselves, and likely die. The council began to adjourn when someone came rushing in, informing the council there were children among the lost. The council reconsidered their vote and decided they must attempt a rescue for the children in the lost group. They decided to send their most seasoned tracker, my guide, in an effort to save those lost in the storm.

He was used to tracking through harsh winter conditions. Each year, he led a small group of men on snowmobile from their village near Victoria Island to Yellowknife, nearly a thousand miles away by land. When possible, he led them over the smoother terrain of frozen lakes. When not on the ice, they faced the rugged terrain of the boreal forest. Once they arrived in Yellowknife, the group gathered a year's worth of supplies for the village. They would repack the sleds, which were dragged behind the snowmobiles, load fuel, and begin the long journey home. There was no room for food. They hunted along the way, surviving off what the forest and tundra offered them.

The council notified our guide of their decision, and he quickly gathered supplies and disappeared on his snowmobile into the blinding storm. In a land void of visual references even in the best of conditions, finding a path through the whiteout blizzard was close to impossible. If his snowmobile stalled and did not quickly re-start, the engine would freeze and he, along with the lost villagers, would freeze to death. Undaunted by the grim odds, he instinctively found his way through sixty miles of whiteout storm and found the lost villagers huddled along the route between the two villages. They were struggling, but alive. They would not have survived the storm. He gathered them together and slowly led everyone, including the children, safely back to the village. One of those rescued was a young girl, who would later become his wife.

This brings me back to the morning I began this chapter with. It was toward the end of the hunt, and the three of us were glassing for caribou. We had already taken three fine caribou bulls and were not looking to take another animal. We really just wanted to watch the migration. Earlier in the day, a wolverine had snuck in on us, within twenty feet, another highlight of the trip. We were all content to just spend the afternoon watching the parade of caribou and talking under the arctic summer sun.

I learned much from our guide, and I felt we had formed a mutual level of trust. As we lay on the soft tundra, leaning into our packs, a peregrine falcon flew low, right over our heads. Peregrine falcons are relatively common where I live in the States, and the sudden sighting seemed a little anticlimactic once I realized the bird of prey was not one of the white gyrfalcons I had been hoping to see. The peregrine had likely migrated thousands of miles from its wintering grounds in South America, crossing life-paths with us for that brief moment. My guide noticed the falcon as well, both of them hunters surviving off the tundra. He talked about the important things in life, like family, food, and shelter. I could feel his excitement and pride as he spoke about the endless bounty the tundra provided him and his family. As I looked around, I saw nothing but barren, flat endlessness. He saw a completely different world, full of opportunity. I was the blind one. He spoke about his people's belief in the spiritual world. I had had similar discussions with the Inuit in western Alaska, where I had been one of the lucky few to access a permit to fly fish the remote Arolik River, a sacred river believed by the local Inuit to be where the spirits of their ancestors live in the form of the wildlife along the waters. As I listened to my guide, I thought about that black arctic fox we had seen earlier in the week. The spiritual connection my dad and I simultaneously felt just a few days before, when we saw that fox and thought of my grandfather, was similar to the connection the Inuit feel on the Arolik in Alaska, or what my guide was describing that afternoon about his village in Nunavut. I believe I understood what he meant and was humbled that he would share his thoughts with me.

The next day, we packed for our return trip to the States. My guide's niece was fascinated to hear about my daughter back home and her love for horses, an animal she had never seen. I wrote down the postal instructions for Nunavut so my daughter could mail her a letter with a picture of her with her horses, which she did. We thanked the family and the lone biologist for their hospitality and hard work. I thanked my guide for sharing his world with me, even for a few brief days. As our floatplane lifted from the cold waters, I strained my neck again, looking out the window. This time, I was looking for landmarks I might recognize around camp or maybe a last sighting of caribou or a bear. As we flew south, I continued to look out the small window. Eventually, there it was, the first tree.

Our bush plane flew low over the increasingly dense forest, and I thought how lucky I was to have met such interesting people. I had just spent a week with a family who not just survives, but thrives in one of the harshest environments on Earth. I became friends with a guy who, every year, rides his snowmobile two thousand miles across the frozen north, relying on nothing but his skills as a hunter to survive. Not to mention meeting the quirky biologist who eats owl. I wished I could hear more of their stories.

As I waited for the next flight out of Yellowknife, I began jotting down notes of the stories and experiences from the week on the back of my plane tickets. Once that white space was filled,

I continued writing on random receipts and papers I found in my carry-on, eventually resorting to scribbles on a few stained, cardboard drink coasters I had swiped from the Black Knight Pub in Yellowknife.

Back home, I thought more about all the guides I had shared remote camps with over the years and their own incredible stories or even just their insightful comments. I once asked a good friend, who guides sheep hunts in Canada, what keeps pushing him to guide in such rough country. We were on horseback, having just traversed an unfriendly mountain range above the snow line, scouting for rams in southern British Columbia, which spit us out an especially nasty drainage. He didn't look over when I posed the question. He kept looking ahead and said finally, "I don't want to go back to the mill." I let that comment go. Other times, I wished I could have spent a whole day exploring the depths of a comment.

On the pancake flat plains of eastern Colorado, my son and I belly crawled a half mile on hard ground, hidden by nothing but dried cow patties, and snuck in on a great antelope. It was a dandy, barely missing Boone & Crockett, and one of the largest taken in that area in a while. We drove the big animal to the ranch owner's house, so they could see their incredible buck. The husband and wife were as old and weathered as the gnarled gray trees in their dusty yard. They walked slowly out the screen door and gave a friendly smile as they bent to look into the bed of the pickup. The rancher's wife nodded approvingly at the big antelope. The old rancher leaned back from the truck and turned to me. "My parents came here on covered wagon," he said, "and I can tell you, that is a good antelope." I wish I could have stayed with him that afternoon. He could have shared a lifetime of great stores, right from their front porch, if I could have stayed longer.

I wanted to share these stories with others, and I spent the next ten years talking to professional outdoorsmen whom I became friends with about their own experiences in the wilderness. They did not have to share these experiences with me, but my interest was sincere, and I always placed our friendship above the importance of any story. Over those years, I had fascinating discussions in remote, wild places with good folks whose friendship I continue to treasure. As often as possible, I recorded my notes of their stories that same day on whatever I could find, usually lying in a sleeping bag with a headlamp to help me see. There were a few times I used a candle. Eventually, I evolved to a smartphone and digitally recorded or typed notes. This was much easier, of course, and less dangerous than a candle. Those notes and recordings eventually became this book.

The book is a collection of stories from guides, outfitters, professional hunters and trappers I have been fortunate to share a few campfires with, and even more fortunate to call my friends. They have lived and worked in the Wrangell Mountains of Alaska, the Wind River Range of Wyoming, the deep bayou of Louisiana, the Everglades of south Florida, the savanna and bushveld of Africa and along the rivers of Central and South America. Each one has a life story that could be its own volume of books. This small collection offers just a glimpse, a few of their stories or comments that made me think, smile, or just shake my head in disbelief.

These stories are not about game hunted or fish caught. They are about everything else a sportsperson experiences in the field: the environment, the weather, other wildlife, and the people—all the "other" incredible things that make a memorable hunting or fishing trip. Some of the stories are difficult to imagine today, but understand that, in many cases, they occurred in a different time and in a sporting world that no longer exists. Some of the species are now thankfully protected and, just as importantly, better understood. What I do know is that very few people appreciate and understand the animals and wilderness where they live as much as those telling the stories in this book.

Hunting is about more than pulling the trigger, and fishing is about more than just landing a fish. They are about immersing oneself in a natural habitat, creating the opportunity for a shot or cast. At its purest, they are experiencing the connection between oneself, the environment, and the game pursued.

These tales are brief. They are harsh, meaningful, and larger than life, just like the people who tell them. That is their simple beauty. I hope you find them as interesting as I do.

AN EARLY CONNECTION

My family lived sustainably off the grid before it was fashionable to do so. My dad had returned from fighting in Vietnam. The country was in recession. We lived on a small farm in rural Upstate New York, where my grandparents had lived before us, and my great-grandparents lived before them. No one in our town had much in terms of material things, including us, but those things were of little importance.

My grandfather and great-grandfather were some of the early fly fishing outfitters in the Catskills. They ran a fishing camp not far from Roscoe, New York, where legendary fly-tying families like the Dettes and Darbees operated their small fly shops, sometimes from the family kitchen. To this day, Dette Trout Flies is the oldest family-run fly shop in the world. Our fishing camp was nestled along the banks of Russell Brook, a small tributary to the famed Beaverkill, which, in turn, feeds the East Branch of the Delaware. This is the birthplace of American fly fishing, our founding waters.

Our small farm was farther upstate, along the Susquehanna River. We were as close to self-sufficient as we could be. Our well water was terrible. It never became an acquired taste, and it stained the sink the same color as the rust that was chewing its way up the floorboards of the family station wagon. Our house had a Vermont Castings wood-burning stove with a chimney out back that we had made by hand with stacked cinder blocks. Our stove sucked all moisture out of the house while maintaining a cozy indoor temperature of about one hundred twelve degrees. My mom, a New York State master gardner, grew squash, tomatoes, beans, radishes, okra, and chives as well as cantaloupe, raspberries, blackberries, and grapes. She grew everything from seed, under special lights in a closet next to our dining room. Once the plants sprouted, they were transplanted into pots littering the kitchen floor. Everything was organic. As a kid, I was jealous of the delicious salty processed foods my friends had the pleasure of eating at their homes. We tapped maple trees for syrup and raised a few hives of bees for honey. It was not unusual while mowing to find our entire colony of bees in some far corner of the yard, hanging from a branch like a living piñata. My dad would come over, cut the branch, and walk it back over to the hive, shaking the bees—most importantly the queen—back into their box.

In the winter, my sister and I had the task of pulling our toboggan across the snowy fields to collect sap from our maple trees. My dad would spend hours in our maple syrup shed, slowly boiling sap over a fire like a moonshiner keeping over his still. He poured the sap from our buckets into a large metal vat, which was built right over the open fire. The sap boiled down to a trace of its former volume into the best maple syrup I have ever tasted. Once we had enough syrup stored in glass jars for the year, including the obligatory gifts for friends and family, he would boil the next batch even farther down, until the syrup turned into a thick, maple butter. This delicious "butter" was a maple honey of the gods. Our syrup supply would last the full year. The maple butter would be gone in a matter of weeks.

Our farm was in the path of Great Lakes-effect weather, and winters were long and cold. In the '70s, our family drove an old, rusted-out Dodge station wagon. The only thing more dangerous than the lack of proper seat belts was the rusted-out floorboard, which sucked most of the exhaust directly into the car. This meant that for our family of four to keep from asphyxiating ourselves during a drive through town, we had to keep the windows rolled down, even in the frigid winter. Sitting in the front seats wasn't so bad. At least you had the heater vent. If you were sitting in the back seat and had recently showered, your wet hair froze into a solid helmet of ice within minutes.

We always seemed to have a wild animal living in the house with us. At one point or another, we had an orphaned opossum, a rehabilitated sparrow hawk, various snakes, a baby groundhog who imprinted me as its mother and followed me everywhere, and a couple of geese named Starsky and Hutch who, as goslings, would nap with me in our hammock out back. We also had a squadron of ducks. I believe we raised ducks as opposed to chickens due to protein value per egg. A duck egg is larger than a chicken egg and contains fifty percent more protein. While this book is a collection of guides' stories, I once heard a fantastic tale about a duck from some bird hunting buddies of mine in Atlanta, which begs repeating.

Years ago, a corporate group from Atlanta was hosting a duck hunt for their clients. The trip required a commercial flight on Eastern Airlines (again, this was years ago …). One of the attending hunters was a well-liked individual, but only had limited experience in the field. The hunt went well enough. Ducks came into the spread, the group got plenty of shots, and limits were taken early. It became time to gather downed mallards that had not yet been retrieved by the dogs. This task was going well until the hunter found an injured duck, which he did not have the heart to finish off. He gathered up the mallard and carefully put it deep within his hunting jacket, determined to take the duck home and rehabilitate it. He carried that duck back to camp, to the airport, past security, and walked right on the plane with the live mallard in his jacket.

The plane took off. Our duck hunter and his duck were seated near the front of the plane. The whole operation would have gone off without a hitch were it not for the airlines' snack service and one of the hunter's buddies, who was sitting in the rear of the plane making loud quacking sounds with his duck call. A stewardess came by and offered peanuts, which the duck hunter accepted and tried to feed his duck. It was only a matter of time. Our hunter ran out of peanuts, his buddy kept quacking from the rear of the plane and all hell broke loose. The duck championed the energy for escape, broke out of the jacket, and flew the entire length of the airplane, shitting all over the passengers. To this day, I am not sure what happened to the duck.

I learned to hunt and fish growing up around our small farm. I took strength in learning from my father that no matter what happened with work, because we could hunt and fish, our family would not go hungry. Field fashion did not exist around our house. My dad would get home from work, leave on his blue buttoned shirt sleeve work shirt, put on a pair of jeans and boots, grab a wool jacket with leftover sixteen-gauge buckshot in the pocket, and pull an old shotgun from the closet as he walked out into the snowy fields behind our barn.

In those days, every one of the guns in our house had been handed down from my grandfather or grandmother. She hunted as well. In fact, one of the shotguns I have to this day is an old, worn Winchester model 1912 my grandmother used to sit on the roof of our house with and shoot pheasant, which lived in the rows of bushes and tall grass separating our yard from the open fields. My dad kept the guns all leaning together in one corner of the small closet in my parents' bedroom. He was not the least bit worried about scratches or dings on the guns. It was a batch of old Winchester, Ithaca, Savage, and Remington rifles and shotguns.

None were fancy. They were all field grade and used hard, the wood stocks darkened from decades of use and rubbing oil after being out in the snow. The shotguns were all old standard sixteen gauge, a rare size to come across today among the more popular twelve and twenty gauges. I still come across old, unopened boxes of sixteen gauge shells among family stuff.

My dad didn't care about the "number of points" on a buck. He hunted those fields and hills behind our house for food. If we were lucky, he would shoot a deer; if unlucky, he would shoot a rabbit. He had me fishing at about three years old. When I was around eight or nine, he introduced me to hunting by simply allowing me to come along. I didn't carry a gun at first. It was never a planned father-son bonding experience. We just did it, and we still do it to this day. I enjoyed fishing from the start. Hunting, which required more patience, especially up north, took more time for me to appreciate.

In my late teens, our family moved from New York to Savannah, Georgia, for a job opportunity my dad had at the port. As I settled into living in Georgia, the crunch of snow and smells of spruce and fresh-cut fescue were replaced by Spanish moss, pine needles, sandy soil, and the smells of paper mills and salt marshes as the comforts of home.

What Georgia opened up immediately for me was a new world of fishing and hunting opportunities. Georgia was really where I learned to hunt. Like most species of wildlife, southern deer are generally smaller in stature than their northern counterparts, who need the bulk and fat to survive harsh winters. In addition, unlike the "still" hunting I grew up with, which effectively means moving slowly through the woods while trying to sneak up on a whitetail, southern styles of hunting included using tree stands placed on the edges of fields or planted food plots. This approach allows you to observe a higher number of animals from the stand, and it conceals movement, both helpful in keeping the interest of young, inexperienced hunters like myself at that time.

I am lucky to have had many sporting mentors over the years, who valued deep knowledge of the outdoors and had the highest regard for ethics and good sportsmanship. This meant not just following the rules, but learning the animals and their habitat so well that you became a selective hunter. By selective, I mean targeting specific mature animals, which have passed their prime breeding age and have begun to decline. One of the first hunting mentors I met in Georgia was Mike Owens.

I met Mike at a hunting club lease in southeast Georgia that my dad and I had joined. Mike is probably the most knowledgeable hunter I know. He taught me how to properly age and judge whitetail deer. One of my early hunting achievements actually had nothing to do with shooting a deer at all. It involved selecting a tree. The property we leased was a little over two thousand acres of planted pine, some wet lowland, and red clay access roads that became as slick as glass after a rain. I scouted much of the property for deer sign and activity and, one day, after finding a promising line of rubs and scrapes, left a climbing stand at the base of a pine tree just off the deer trail. This was short-sighted and lazy on my part. I should have carried the climber back out of the woods once I found my tree. That night at camp, Mike asked who had left their climbing stand out in the woods, to which I confessed. Mike later came up to me and said, "If someone put a new chair in your living room, would you notice that?" I replied that yes, I would. "Well," Mike said, "that's what you did when you left your climber at the base of that tree. That buck now knows someone was in his living room." It was great advice, and it fundamentally changed my approach to hunting from that day forward. However, if I am being honest, part of me was also excited to think that on over two thousand acres of planted pine, I had scouted and picked the same tree as Mike.

Mike is also the one who introduced me to big game hunting in Canada, which eventually led me to many of the guides and outfitters I have befriended over the years. Mike had previously hunted with a well-known outfitter named Jim Shockey. One year, Mike invited me to join him on one of his hunting trips to Shockey's deer camp in northern Saskatchewan. To prepare for the trip, Mike did an outstanding job of scaring me to death about the ramifications of shooting an immature or small buck. One of the challenges of hunting a new location, where deer differ in body structure, is judging body size. The same mature buck you are used to seeing in Georgia that weighs one hundred seventy-five pounds may weigh two hundred seventy-five pounds in Canada. Mike armed me with a library of reference books and videos on aging and judging northern and southern whitetail deer, which I studied intently for a year prior to the trip.

Shockey's deer camp was an old curling rink, which had been renovated into a hunting camp. One of the other hunters in camp that week was an ex-football player from Alabama. He unknowingly had brought a black widow spider all the way from Alabama to Saskatchewan in his hunting boot, which bit him on the foot the first morning in camp. He saw a local doctor who confirmed he would be fine, but the intense pain from the bite kept him chair-bound most of the week, a reminder of how powerful the bite can be from that small spider, even to an ex-linebacker.

My guide was a knowledgeable and extremely pleasant fellow with a wizened Gandalf beard. His name was Brian Wojciechowski, or "Wojo," for short. I don't know why, but I called him Brian. I was singularly focused on, and candidly scared about, shooting the wrong deer and probably did not feel cool enough yet to yell out "Wojo!" November weather in Northern Saskatchewan is unpredictable. As a deer hunter, you wish for freezing cold to keep deer up and moving, especially during the breeding season, or rut. That week, we got our wish, with subzero temperatures every day.

I hunted all day every day, sitting in a ground blind, which was a small canvas tent. Brian would drive me out to the blind before sunrise each morning on a four-wheeler. He would then pick me up each evening after dark. I took a bottle to pee in, which froze within minutes, and a small cooler. The cooler was not to keep things cool; it was to keep a sandwich and drink bottle from freezing solid. The first morning, Brian gave me explicit instruction to never leave the blind unless he was there, even if I shot a deer. If you got lost in the dark woods, you could easily freeze to death. Worse were the timber wolves, which were enormous, over seven feet in length. Twice in the evening, I heard the wolves close around me in the woods, while waiting for Brian's four-wheeler lights in the dark.

I ended up taking a big-bodied whitetail that week, which weighed close to three hundred pounds. The antlers were not overly impressive by Saskatchewan standards, but it was a good mature buck. And it was my first of what would be many Canadian big game animals. Jim Shockey's operations are quite involved with local food shelters and programs to share the meat with those in need. Once we got my deer back to camp and started butchering the animal, Brian placed a call to a local food shelter. Thirty minutes later, a rusted-out station wagon came rumbling up the road. Every time it hit a pothole, a few inches of sidewall fell from the car. The wagon pulled up, and a tired-looking younger woman stepped out. She was a single mom with three or four kids, all piled in the back seat. We loaded the back of her car with enough venison to feed her family for the entire winter, and then some. She never said a word, but as she was getting back in the car, she stared at me deeply. Her eyes said it all. She had plenty of things to worry about in her life, but feeding her kids that winter would not be one of them.

Brian and I quickly connected as guide and hunter. Brian had the knowledge, of course, but we both had a similar quiet, patient, yet focused approach to hunting. At some point during the hunt Brian asked me if I would have any interest in joining him at Shockey's camp on Vancouver Island to hunt some of the largest black bear on Earth, the coastal bear of British Columbia. I should note, the heaviest black bear anywhere come from the rural wheat, corn, and peanut fields of eastern North Carolina, just a few hours east of where I live today. Brian mentioned how they processed the bear meat for use in Vancouver area shelters, which, again, I was interested in and found to be very true after we harvested bear.

His invitation to go bear hunting sparked a memory. When I was a kid back on the farm in New York, my dad had told me one snowy afternoon, while sitting in front of that wood-burning blast furnace in our family room, that he hoped to be able to go bear hunting one day. Twenty-five years later, I remembered his comment, and I invited him to join Brian and me to chase his bear on Vancouver Island.

Northern Vancouver Island is mountainous dense forest covered with logging roads. Brian, my dad, and I hunted the exposed slopes and logging tracks, glassing for bear. One afternoon, we were high up on a logging road, not far from where a mountain lion crossed in front of us just a few days before. Our vantage revealed an enormous valley and expansive mountain range. Our field of view was easily over one hundred square miles of wilderness. As I was glassing the view with binoculars, something barely visible on a distant mountainside caught my eye. It was a small piece of culvert pipe that had broken off under a distant logging road. The piece of culvert could not have been more than a few feet long, but the recess inside the pipe happened to be in shadow at that moment, creating a tiny spec of pitch black among the douglas fir, which, even from our great distance, somewhat resembled the hindquarter of a black bear.

The single best piece of hunting advice I ever received was from my grandfather. He had given it to my father, who passed it along to me. I have since passed it down to both my son and daughter. My grandfather's advice was this: "Don't look for an animal; look for an ear." What my grandfather meant was that the animal is part of the natural surroundings, and if you only look for the animal's entire body, you may miss seeing the animal entirely.

That distant black culvert wasn't an ear, but my grandfather's theory still applied. I was curious if my dad would spot the same needle in a haystack. I put my binoculars down and asked him to look out in the general direction I had been glassing and to tell me if he saw anything that stood out. A minute later, with his binoculars still up to his eyes, he said, "Yep, I see a small piece of pipe on that far mountain that kind of looks like the rear end of a bear." The connection to our natural surroundings that my grandfather had instilled in both of us was there.

That "connection" to the outdoors lives within everyone in this book. One of my close hunting friends from Atlanta, whom I effectively consider a guide since he has probably helped teach a hundred people to hunt and fish over the years, is a guy named Steele Hawkins. Steele has that "connection" to the outdoors as deep as anyone I know.

Steele grew up near the Santee Cooper Lakes of South Carolina. The lakes are famous for largemouth bass and enormous catfish. The lakes are fed by the Congaree River, which quietly forms a band of remote wilderness between Columbia and Charleston. Along its flow, the Congaree nurtures a vast flood plain, home to deep cypress swamps and one of the largest remaining tracts of old-growth hardwood trees in the United States. To the west of the Congaree flows the Savannah River. The Savannah forms much of the boundary between South Carolina and Georgia while slowly draining the southeastern Appalachian Mountains. Before it reaches the brackish marshes and shipping channel near Savannah, the river floods endless remote swampland. The swamps of the Savannah River are deep and dangerous and hold secrets; they are, as is the title of author and naturalist James Kilgo's memoir, *Deep Enough for Ivorybills.*

I describe these swamps to describe Steele. Steele has spent his life exploring the Congaree and Savannah River swamps. He is fundamentally connected to them. Like Mike Owens, I met Steele at a hunting club, this one near Covington, Georgia, not far from Atlanta. When I first met Steele, he asked me if I was interested in arrowheads. I was interested in arrowheads, but even more interested in who would actually ask me that question. I liked him immediately.

Steele looks like the guy at the bar you want to avoid. He is of average height, but built like the thick trunk of a tree. I am not quite sure where Steele's neck ends and his shoulders begin. He is just big all around. His father, Alex Hawkins, played on the legendary Baltimore Colts teams of the late 1950s and early '60s. Steele and I hunted the Savannah River swamps together. I would be wearing full scent-free camo and high rubber boots. Steele would wear shorts and a sweaty Hawaiian shirt that looked like it had not been washed in years. He might have worn old sneakers or maybe gone barefoot. Either way, Steel would shoot more deer and hogs than any of us. No amount of high-tech gear replaces woodsmanship.

Years after I met him, I got a call late one night. I immediately recognized Steele's grizzled voice, and I could tell he was upset. "I can see the sky," he told me. I listened but didn't understand what he was trying to say. "I looked, and I saw the sky," he repeated. It took a few more minutes for him to compose what he was trying to say. "I looked for the big tree, and it wasn't there," he said dejectedly.

Steele was referring to an old water oak on our property. It was one of the oldest and largest water oaks in the country. Arborists from the University of Georgia had even come to see the incredible tree. Water oaks are not long-lived trees, but they can become quite massive. A damaging windstorm had blown through central

Georgia a few days prior, spawning powerful wind shear that blew over the colossal tree. That bear of a man was reduced to tears by the death of that tree.

The following week, I drove down to see Steele and the tree. The opening created by the lost leaf canopy was remarkable. There was expansive sky where, before, a massive tree had stood. The tree lay on its side. Branches over six feet in diameter were driven into the ground, and the root ball, later measured at nearly twenty feet in diameter, stood ugly and dismembered, having erupted from the earth, breaking its connection with us. That connection to the outdoors goes beyond just shooting and casting; in this case, it had to do with losing a special tree. To Steele, it was like losing a friend.

BIG FISH

As I mentioned earlier, I learned to fish before learning to hunt. A fascination which probably began in the 1970s when I watched the shark fishermen at Jeannette's Pier near Nags Head on North Carolina's Outer Banks.

Some of my friends grew up fishing for and eating snapper, grouper, flounder, or other delicious white, flaky fish. I did not. My family ate prodigious amounts of bluefish, a dark, strong-flavored fish that did not seem to become lighter and milder as advertised when cooked.

In the 1960s and '70s, my grandparents explored back roads of the east coast, travelling between the farm in New York and Florida, where my great-grandparents had moved. One of their routes took them along the Outer Banks of North Carolina, where my grandfather recognized the incredible saltwater fishing opportunities. They befriended the owners of a local motel, as well as the local bait shop called "Tatum's Tackle" near Nags Head. This began what would become a twenty-year family tradition of chasing the bluefish runs along the Outer Banks.

Each fall and spring, we would drive eight hours from the farm to the Outer Banks, loaded with fishing gear, fish hard all week, pack our bluefish in ice coolers, and haul them back up north.

The bluefish fillets joined the frozen venison, rabbit, turkey, or anything else my dad had harvested on our property in the freezer. We then ate bluefish every day until it was gone and would do it again the next season. I don't care to eat bluefish again.

In those years, the blues hit the Outer Banks in the cold months of November and April, ensuring fast action from the surf and frozen fingers and wet jeans if you were not lucky enough to own a pair of heavy chest waders. As an eight- or nine-year-old kid, I could barely hold up a pair of the old, heavy rubber or canvas waders, which were taller than I was. We fished from Nags Head down to Rodanthe, following fisherman's chatter on the CB radio. "The blues are running!" was thrilling to hear over the static, causing havoc for those listening. If the fast-moving schools were hitting the beach up at Nags Heads, we would chase them on foot, watching the black slicks of bait get pushed up on shore by the chopper blues. In those days, you could see the mass of big blues crashing above the water's surface and attacking hapless baitfish like frenzied wolves. The equipment was simple: a towering surf rod, stiff enough to launch a three- or four-ounce weighted silver Hopkins plug with a treble hook as far out as you could cast.

If the blues were running farther south, near Oregon Inlet or down toward Rodanthe, we found public access points and drove right out on the beach to chase the schools. The pace was hectic. Rushed fingers, stiff with cold, desperately trying to untangle line knots to make one more cast before the crashing school disappeared. This typically ended in frustration, mistakes, and endless cursing. There is something about seeing a crashing school of fish on the surface that brings out the nerves, or buck fever, in all of us.

I remember the old fishermen, many from the Northeast, heaving those heavy plugs out beyond the first row of breakers. The more dedicated among them would walk out through the crashing surf, to cast from the second breakers. The blue fishermen were a breed apart: heavy canvas or rubber waders above the chest, a flannel shirt soaked with salt spray, and a worn baseball hat. If they were lucky, an idling four-wheel-drive pickup, with a grand organ of rod holders welded to the front bumper, could provide a quick reprieve from the bitter cold of the salt water and wind. There were few trophy pictures taken, but the grins were wide and the coolers were heavy with fish, dark bluefish tails sticking out each end, hardened stiff and sharp.

Sometimes we stopped by the fishing piers. The piers up by Kitty Hawk and Nags Head were postcard-friendly places with brightly colored T-shirts and pinball machines. Jennette's Pier, down by Whale-Bone Junction, across from Sam & Omies bar, was something else. Jennette's Pier was rebuilt after being destroyed by Hurricane Isabel in the early 2000s and, today, is a beautiful, sturdy facility. In the late '70s and early '80s, however, Jennette's was old, dark, sea-battered, and worn.

Jennette's was where the shark fisherman went. Black and white photos of huge sharks caught by the pier fishermen littered the cluttered walls of the tiny bait and tackle shop, the corners of the photos yellowed by patina of old cellophane tape. As a young kid, I was fascinated with those pictures. Massive sharks hanging from old ropes, their bodies grotesquely stretched and swollen by gravity pulling their stomach and liver downward toward unnaturally extended jaws. The jaws always looked wet and bloody, even in black and white. This was right around the time the movie *Jaws* came out, land-locking a generation of swimmers and transforming sharks into monsters.

The shark fishermen fished late at night, out at the very end of the pier. Their dim lights beckoned to a place you felt you should not go. I remember walking out the pier at night as a kid. The old, battered wooden pier shuddered when big swells rolled in. At the end of the pier, the shark fishermen's short, stiff rods with heavy chrome reels leaned against the handrail like baseball bats. The wooden handrails were sticky and soft, tenderized by years of sea spray and being sliced up by bait-cutting knives. The fishermen sat under dim lights on coolers of ice, beer, and bait, lost in their own thoughts, facing away into the blackness of the cold Atlantic. They used tuna heads for bait, with giant hooks tied to heavy gauge wire, or even chain leaders. The short, heavy shark rods were not made for casting, and the bait was attached to balloons or inflated trash bags, lowered from the pier and allowed to float out with the tide. Sometimes one of the fishermen had the harrowing job of rowing the bait out into the dark, choppy waters in a small boat.

Luke Donat is a flounder fishing guide I was introduced to by a mutual friend, Seth Vernon, whom I write about in the next chapter. I recently fished with Luke near the mouth of the Cape Fear River, south of Wilmington, North Carolina. It had been raining heavily the previous week, and the coastal salt waters were inundated with fresh water runoff, making for poor fishing conditions. So, we spent the day exploring the coastal waters and talking. Like myself, Luke grew up fishing the Outer Banks. I am a good bit older than Luke, but learned that afternoon that we had fished many of the same places as kids, including Jennette's Pier, and had similar memories.

As a kid, Luke was also fascinated with the shark fishermen out at the end of Jennette's pier. He recalled one evening in particular. The unlucky fisherman chosen to row the bait out that night only had a small inflatable raft. He rowed from the beach to the end of the pier, where his buddies lowered their fishing lines with bloody tuna heads down into the dingy. He then rowed out into the black ocean, leaving a slick chum line of oily tuna blood behind the raft as he rowed. Right about the time he disappeared into the dark, a huge shark hit the back of the raft so hard it capsized and deflated the small boat. Luke recalls hearing yells and strange sounds out beyond the end of the pier in the darkness. The fishermen up on the pier began leaning over the rail, yelling down toward the water.

Their friend suddenly appeared, swimming frantically in the dark waves. He swam straight to the pier, grabbed the nearest barnacle-covered piling and started shimmying himself up. He was lucky to have made it back to the pier with no damage, other than to his chest and legs, which were ripped to shreds by the pier barnacles as he clawed his way out of the water. I guess he still had to swim back to the beach.

Jennette's Pier was legendary in those days among shark fishermen. Buz Boetticher's dusky shark weighed 575 pounds. According to the old stories, Buz had had the job of rowing out the bait earlier that night and, upon returning to the pier, mentioned to his buddies he was sure he had felt the small boat rise as an unseen huge fish pushed water from below. Bob Keller's dusky shark weighed 610 pounds, and a monstrous hammerhead was later caught off the pier, tipping the scales at over 700 pounds.[1]

The Carolinas' most legendary shark was probably Walter Maxwell's 1,780-pound tiger shark caught in 1964 from the Cherry Grove pier, just north of Myrtle Beach, South Carolina. Interestingly, a few years later, Mr. Maxwell was fighting another huge tiger; this one he estimated to be 1,200 pounds. While he was fighting the tiger, a bigger shark, the biggest Mr. Maxwell said he had ever seen, attacked it, taking a thirty-six-inch bite out of the fish. Based on bite radius measurements, the shark that attacked Mr. Maxwell's tiger was estimated at 3,500 pounds. It sounded impossible. Local fishermen thought it must have been a giant great white but, at that time, most people didn't associate the southeastern United States with great white sharks.

Following college, I opted to delay working as long as I could and decided instead to put myself through business school. The irony being, to pay for grad school, I had to work three jobs. While at school, even though I was a business major, I jumped at an opportunity to spend a semester abroad studying ecology, specifically the effects of deforestation, at a small, remote, field school in the rainforests of Queensland, Australia.

Of course, Australia is also famous for big sharks. One of the more incredible stories I came across was of a monstrous shark that had bitten a twelve-foot great white in half. The coastal town of Cairns (pronounced "Cans") was a few hours, an easy hitchhike, from my school. Cairns is a mecca among blue-water billfishermen, in the same vein as Cape Hatteras, Hawaii, Cabo San Lucas, and Panama. I spent as much time in Cairns as I could. Not that I had any money to fish offshore ... I didn't. I just liked being around such a legendary fishing place, and for a few bucks a night, I could stay at the hostel down by the water.

One afternoon, I heard a shark fisherman had what was left of a twelve-foot white shark, which had been caught in southern Australia and brought up to a town not far from Cairns in a big freezer-trailer. The big shark had been bitten in two by a larger shark as it was being reeled in. I hitchhiked to the coastal town, found the fisherman, and waited all day while he and his mates cleaned fish. After they finished their work, he took me to see what was left of the great white in the freezer. Sure enough, on the floor of the trailer was half of a great white shark, at one time over twelve feet long. The half-moon shaped bite behind the dorsal fin told the story. The unseen fish, likely a more massive great white, had been big enough to bite a twelve-footer cleanly in half.

In the early '70s, Montauk, New York, located at the very tip of Long Island, was the epicenter of big shark fishing. In those days, fishermen from all over the world traveled to Montauk to battle giant thresher, mako, and even great white sharks. They loved catching makos, for the desirable meat and aerial acrobatics when hooked, but what they really wanted to find was a great white, and the fisherman best known for finding great whites was Frank Mundus, captain of the *Cricket II*.

Frank Mundus's shark-fishing career began with chasing bluefish. His charters would lose bluefish to sharks as they were being reeled in, and he soon realized that fishermen would pay to battle the bigger fish. He coined the phrase "Monster Fishing" and began chartering fishing trips, targeting giant sharks, which would be "chummed" in using chunks of oily fish, pilot whale, or even basking shark. One of Captain Mundus's more famous clients was Peter Benchley, author of *Jaws*, who was rumored to have based the character Quint on Frank Mundus himself.

One of the scenes from the movie Frank Mundus later noted as inaccurate was when Quint was boiling shark jaws in his shack. Mundus noted that, when boiled, shark jaws dissolve and all you have left are the teeth. When I was in my late teens, right after my family moved to Savannah, I began fishing for sharks. The sharks I caught along the Georgia coast would have been toothpicks for the Montauk sharks, but I was determined to have a set of jaws, just like the movie. So I boiled my first set of jaws in our family kitchen. Hours later, I opened the pot and pulled out a wad of dissolved slime with a few loose teeth.

I was recently fly fishing for false albacore, a small tuna, near Cape Lookout on the Outer Banks of North Carolina. Each fall, "albies," as they are called, follow baitfish along the barrier islands and inlets of the Core and Shackleford Banks and iconic Cape Lookout. The legendary home base for this annual "epic" fishing is Harkers Island. Harkers Island is at the end of the road. The island breathes of fishing and waterfowl history. Even the short, wind-shaped trees that cover the island tell stories of past storms and resilient people. About halfway down the main road is Harkers Island Fishing Center, which, for over thirty years, has been run by Rob Pasfield. Rob is a welcoming and unassuming guy who has as much experience on the water as anyone I have fished with. You don't go to Harkers Island for luxury; you go to experience some of the most incredible fishing available along the eastern coast.

On this particular trip, my guide, a personal friend, had gotten sick and could not go out. Rob offered to take me, a generous offer from a captain who was probably enjoying his first day off in weeks. We quickly found schools of albies and landed a few on fly. As we searched for more albies, I asked Rob where he had lived prior to coming to Harkers Island. He said he used to live up by Long Island and fished out of Montauk. This caught my attention, and I asked if he had ever worked on some of the old boats that used to go after the big sharks. Rob said, "When I was young, in my late teens, I was a mate for a guy named Frank Mundus on a boat called the *Cricket II*."

I couldn't believe I was fishing with one of the mates from that boat. To be honest, I think Rob couldn't believe I had ever heard of Frank Mundus or the *Cricket II*. That afternoon, while albie fishing, as I listened to Rob telling me some of the old stories, scenes from the movie kept coming to mind. Rob noted they had fished for both shark and big tuna, but the shark fishing charters were always an overnight excursion. On bigger fish, Rob sometimes had the dangerous job of harpooning them from the plank extending out from the bow. "When you harpoon a really big shark, the tail can whip up and can slap the plank, which could be scary," Rob said. He added that when a hooked fish is jumping, like a mako shark, they will tire themselves out quickly, but the fish that dive keep fighting longer. Sometimes they would fasten barrels to the really big, harpooned sharks to keep them from diving. The ropes connected to the barrels would then be hooked to the winch at the base of the mast, and the *Cricket II* would be pulled slowly sideways in the water by the massive shark.

"Frank Mundus was a real character," Rob recalled. One evening a small group of well-dressed Manhattan socialites was out visiting the Hamptons. They had driven to Montauk for a seafood dinner and could not find the restaurant. The first "locals" they found to ask for direction were Frank Mundus and Rob, who were both sitting low in the bed of a pickup truck near the docks, their bodies obstructed from view. Frank and Rob were completely soaked in turtle blood. That afternoon, as the *Cricket II* returned to the docks, one of the commercial netters mistakenly killed a sea turtle in the nets. Not wanting to waste the animal, the netters brought the turtle back to the docks and offered the meat to Frank, who gladly accepted. They lifted the huge turtle, upside down, into the back of Frank's pick-up, where he and Rob began cutting out the meat. Of course, the upside down turtle shell formed a giant bowl filled with blood, soaking both of them from their feet to elbows. As the delicate party of black tuxedos and evening dresses approached the truck, Frank took great pleasure … in standing up.

Rob told me about another time Frank's neighbor asked him for help in getting rid of some raccoons that had moved into his chimney. Frank walked over to the neighbor's house with a shotgun, stuck the barrel of the gun up the chimney, and pulled the trigger. A pile of dead raccoons fell down into the fireplace, including one kit, or baby, that was still alive. Well, Frank kept the kit and raised it on the *Cricket II*. "That raccoon was like our mascot," Rob said while smiling. "One day, out on a charter, we couldn't find the raccoon. We looked all over the boat. Suddenly, one of the fishermen started screaming. It turned out the raccoon had fallen into the bilge pump and covered itself with oil. It then climbed out of the bilge, crawled up the tower, and leapt onto the back of one of the fishermen. It was slimy, black, and didn't even look like a raccoon. They were all screaming," he laughed.

Rob and I had a great day of fishing, and we caught several nice albies on fly. Around midday, Rob spotted a huge pod of crashing fish and diving birds about five hundred yards ahead of our boat. Personally, I was diving into a bag of chips. Depending on the type of bait they are chasing, albies may only stay on the surface for a few brief moments. This was the biggest school we had seen all day, and we were racing toward it when my chip bag got caught in the wind and went flying out of my hand. At first, neither of us said anything, but I felt sick that I had been so careless. I could tell Rob felt bad, too, and the idea of leaving that empty plastic bag was really bothering him. So, after a few more seconds, we both decided to forget the school of fish and turn around to go look for the plastic bag. Sure enough, there it was, floating high like a Portuguese man o' war jellyfish full of air. I scooped up the bag, and we continued looking for fish. Like all the guides in this book, Rob has a deep connection to the outdoors, and even for a guy who used to hunt for four-thousand-pound sharks, he wanted to protect his waters from that small plastic bag.

Today, great white sharks are thankfully protected, and thanks to video documentaries, the public has a new appreciation for this amazing animal. Quite a change from those old black and white photos of dead sharks forty years ago. New hot spots for great white activity are where you can observe the shark, not catch it. Places like the Farallon Islands off the coast of San Francisco, Hawaii, and the coast of Baja. South Africa is also near the top of the list of places to observe great whites, although as of the publication of this book, great white sightings in South Africa had dropped. Marine biologists are studying various causes possibly responsible for the decline, including the possibility that the white sharks are being attacked by orcas, who enjoy shark liver.

I knew from seeing those old fishing pictures as a kid that the southeastern US coast was home to big tiger sharks and hammerheads, but I did not know about the great whites. There is something pure about being in an environment with a top predator. I don't know if you feel more alive, or just more awake. The first time I saw a brown bear footprint was about twenty-five years ago on the coast of western Alaska. I was holding nothing but a fly rod, and seeing the giant bear print next to my smaller wading boot was a wake-up call that I wasn't in the land of coyotes and bobcats anymore. Needless to say, I was as surprised as anyone to learn one of the top new locations for great white activity in the world is the southeastern United States. I suppose they have always been here; we just never realized it until researchers started tagging white sharks and tracking their movement along the eastern seaboard via satellite.

Luke Donat, whom I mentioned earlier, had quite an experience with a great white while flounder fishing. Depending on current and tide, Luke pursues flounder in the Wilmington, North Carolina area, everywhere from the Cape Fear River, to the marshes along the Intercoastal Waterway to the open saltwater bays and ocean.

Around 2015, Luke was flounder fishing a few hundred yards off the coast near Wilmington. As he was letting lines out, he noticed birds working schools of fish farther up the beach. He idled his boat over for a closer look. As he approached, he saw vast schools of pogies (a coastal baitfish) hitting the surface, some of the biggest pogies Luke had ever seen. As he watched the frantic schools, they pooled into massive bait balls, ebbing and flowing like lava lamps under the surface. Baitfish form these tight schools to confuse and evade larger predators which, in this case, turned out to be huge schools of eighty- to one-hundred-pound tarpon and forty- and fifty-pound redfish. The tarpon and redfish crashed into the balls of pogies in frenzied runs, an incredible sight, just a few hundred yards from shore in twenty-one feet of water.

As Luke watched this amazing scene of nature unfold, a larger dark shape was moving slowly around his boat. Luke thought it had to be another big mass of pogies. He watched the dark shape come closer, getting within ten yards of his boat. There was something different about the way it moved, and he realized it wasn't a school—it was a single massive fish. It was the biggest shark Luke had ever seen. At first, he thought it must be a great big tiger shark, but it did not have the tell-tale vertical patterns. The giant shark came alongside Luke's boat, and its meter-high dorsal fin broke the surface. It was an enormous great white. The big pogies had attracted the tarpon and bull reds. The tarpon and reds had attracted the great white. The fin passed just yards from Luke's boat. Attached to the fin was a tag and tracking device. Luke noted the identification data on the tag and later called in the information. It was one of the great whites being tracked via satellite by Ocearch, a shark research group. The researchers identified the shark as Mary Lee, a huge female, and confirmed from their tracking data that she was indeed off the coast of Wilmington.

Luke's flounder boat was eighteen feet long with a design that weighs approximately 1,500 pounds. Assuming he was running a 150-horsepower outboard, the engine weighed approximately 500 pounds. Combined, Luke's presence was eighteen feet long and weighed approximately 2,000 pounds. Based on data provided by Ocearch, Mary Lee was bigger. Female great whites grow significantly larger than the males. Mary Lee had been tagged and weighed in 2012 at sixteen feet in length and more than 3,400 pounds. A few years later, when Luke saw her, she would have been even larger. Incredibly, Mary Lee's girth and dorsal fin took up a third or more of the water depth where Luke had spotted her. You never know what you are going to see on a day in the woods or on the water. That day, Luke went fishing for flounder and found a three-and-a-half-thousand-pound great white.

The batteries on the shark tracking devices have a five-year life, and Mary Lee's device went silent in 2017. Hopefully, Mary Lee is still patrolling the eastern coast of the United States. Looking back, with the knowledge we have today that these top predators call the southeastern coast of the US home, it turns out Mr. Maxwell's story could well have been right. The tiger shark he hooked off the North Carolina coast in the 1960s could indeed have been attacked by a fish that weighed 3,500 pounds.

COASTAL GUIDE

ollowing grad school, I married a girl from another small
town in Upstate New York with a mutual love for the
outdoors and who, surprisingly, put up with my hunting
and fishing exploits. Sue and I raised our kids in Atlanta, Georgia,
and did our best to balance my job in commercial real estate and
life in the suburbs with escaping to the outdoors. During those
years, I fly fished the southern Appalachian Mountains and
Florida coasts extensively. As our kids entered high school, we
moved from Atlanta to a small town in horse country south of
Charlotte, North Carolina, where we live today.

I had dreamed of living in North Carolina since I was a kid
chasing those bluefish up and down the Outer Banks. I knew the
coastal waters of North Carolina's northern outer banks were
legendary for coastal inshore and offshore blue water fishing as
well as waterfowl hunting, but, at that time, I knew very little
about the barrier islands to the south, from Ocracoke Island,
down along the Core and Shackleford Banks, all the way to the
extensive fishery around Wilmington and the Cape Fear River.

One of the first things I did after we had settled into our new
home in the Carolinas was begin researching fly fishing guides
near Wilmington, the closest coastal area to where we lived. More

and more, the name Seth Vernon kept coming up. I finally called Seth and introduced myself. As with every introduction, you get an immediate first impression. I liked Seth right away. He didn't talk about all the fish he caught, or how big, and he never promised any expectations. Instead, he enthusiastically spoke about the region and the fishery. I booked a trip with him on the spot, and we have since become fast friends.

Seth's knowledge of the region's ecosystem goes far beyond fly fishing. A day with Seth, poling the shallow marsh grass on a tailing tide looking for redfish, is an education in more than *Sciaenops ocellatus*. Our first discussion on his flats boat was supposed to be about redfishing. Instead, we talked about pursuing the prehistoric bowfin fish on fly rod in the tannic waters of the Black River in southeastern North Carolina, home to some of the oldest living bald cypress trees in the world. His family is from the Louisiana bayou. As a self-proclaimed "Coonass," or person of Cajun ethnicity, Seth is fascinated with regional linguistics. For example, Seth taught me that, in the bayou, the peregrine falcon is a *duck hawk*, the osprey is a *fish hawk*, and the red-shouldered hawk is a *chicken hawk*. Also, the word *alligator* was originally lost in translation. Evidently, early Spanish explorers called alligators "el lagarto" or "the lizard." English settlers mistakenly heard "alligator."

Seth is no stranger to big sharks. He has reminded me how large the big tigers get along the Carolina coast and how they adjust their feeding patterns to various habitats. Tiger sharks are known for preying on sea turtles, but will eat whatever happens to be abundant in the area. Seth told me that years ago, a big tiger shark was caught off of Hilton Head Island, South Carolina, and weighed about a thousand pounds. When they cut open the shark's stomach, they found over a hundred pounds of shrimp inside. The big tiger shark had been swimming around the marshes of Hilton Head, straining shrimp like a plankton-eating basking shark.

A few years ago, two of Seth's spearfishing pals were preparing to free dive off of Wilmington. As they prepared for the first dive, they spotted an enormous great white. Seth's buddies gave the shark wide berth and relocated to a new dive position a full fifteen miles away. They were only moments into the dive at the new location when two more great whites appeared ... three great white sharks in one afternoon.

While Seth's fishing stories of coastal waters are extensive, my favorite stories are about his family in the bayou, specifically his grandfather. "He lived a full life," Seth said proudly of his grandfather. Seth and I were sitting on his flats boat in the marsh behind Wrightsville Beach, North Carolina. The Intracoastal Waterway was not far behind us. There was an incoming weather front, which made for a slow day of red fishing but was perfect for hanging out on his flats boat, listening to stories about his grandfather.

James Elon Vernon, Jr. was born and raised in Baton Rouge, Louisiana. He lived in Capital Heights, just a few blocks from LSU and Mike the Tiger. Seth recalled a story about driving through town in his grandfather's F100 pickup. "We pulled up to this country store. There was an old, blind black man sitting on the porch. I remember he looked so wise with his white hair and beard. As my grandfather shut his truck door, the old man said, 'Hey, Rouge!' My grandfather yelled back 'hello.' The old, blind man had recognized the sound of my grandfather's truck door!" Seth exclaimed. He continued, "When I was a kid, I never understood why everyone called him 'Rouge.'" It turned out he was so nicknamed because of his flaming red hair when he was younger. "I only knew my granddad with white hair."

Seth grew up hunting and fishing with his grandfather. His granddad had a large duck hunting camp out in the bayou delta he leased from one of the gas companies. They used floating barges with trailers as a camp. Seth's uncle lived in a land-based camp on the Amite River, a beautiful slow-moving river covered with flooded cypress trees and Spanish moss, which flows into Lake Maurepas and eventually Lake Pontchartrain near New Orleans. The Amite River is loaded with alligators and other prehistoric creatures. One afternoon, the Vernon family was water skiing on the river. Seth's sister was on the skis. Seth's dad looked back from driving the boat to check on her. Right behind his sister, following in the wake, was a giant alligator gar. The huge fish wasn't trying to attack his sister. It was swimming in the wake behind the boat, shaking its huge alligator head back and forth out of the water as it snapped at baitfish and minnows being kicked up by the boat.

"My uncle and grandfather would catch alligator gar and catfish on catfish rigs tied off to a cyprus tree," Seth told me. "They only fished the alligator gar if they got a permit." If they caught a gar, they would bring it back to camp and butcher it. "They rolled that flaky, boney gar meat to get the good meat out of it." Once they had the good meat, they would soak it to remove the nasty gar flavor, then cover it in breading, roll it up into ball-shaped patties, and deep-fry it. "Alligator gar balls are the size of a softball, and they are a Cajun mainstay," Seth told me. "It wasn't for bait; they ate it and loved it … it was terrible."

As a kid, Seth jumped at the opportunity to hang out with his grandfather. "He took me fishing when no one else would take me fishing," Seth recalled fondly of his grandfather. "He would take me out in the bayou or swamp from dawn to dusk. He was a sportsman, a real swamp rat." One afternoon, he took Seth fishing and a moccasin fell from a tree into their small outboard jon boat. Seth pushed back away from the snake. His grandfather calmly reached down, grabbed the moccasin by the tail, and threw it back in the water. "Was that a dangerous one?" young Seth asked. His granddad smiled at him and said in his deep Cajun accent, "Yeah, baby!"

The duck camp down in the bayou was for wildfowling, but his uncle's "Fish Camp" up on the Amite was where they hunted and fished. "They had dogs everywhere, Catahoula dogs, nasty little cur dogs," said Seth. Seth asked his uncle one day why he had so many three-legged dogs. His uncle would look out at the river and point to an alligator. "That's why." The dogs were their security detail. According to Seth, if anyone was in the woods who was not supposed to be there, there would be loose dogs to warn him. "They ran along the river barking at the alligators. Every once in a while, a gator would grab a hold of one of the dogs and, if it escaped, it would lose a leg." Seth's uncle used to keep pigs at the camp as well. When the alligator numbers started to increase in the river, he lost more and more hogs. Seth added, "He finally couldn't keep hogs because of the gators."

Seth's grandfather and uncle hunted alligator on the Amite River for food. "They hunted big gators, nuisance gators, in season and out of season when they needed the meat," Seth told me. They hunted alligator from a small jon boat with steel harpoons and giant treble hooks. "They would snag gators under the armpit with big treble hooks attached to long wire leaders, bring them up to the boat, and shoot them with a single-shot .22-caliber rifle." They also used steel harpoons. "They would harpoon the alligator off the beach. The harpoon was tied to a long cord, which the alligator would wrap itself up in when it started rolling. That would tire out the gator. Then they could bring it up to the boat and finish it off."

"It was important to tire out the gator before you brought it in," Seth added. "You don't bring a green gator in the boat."

Early one morning, Seth's grandfather and a neighbor, Mr. Brumfield, were running their Go Devil outboard swamp boat to their duck blind and hit a giant gator in the water. The boat overturned, they lost their guns, and Mr. Brumfield almost drowned. "They were always having run-ins with alligator, snakes, wild hogs … my cousin Taylor got hooked by a boar's tusk and they had to sew him up back at Fish Camp," Seth told me. "They used Jack Daniels as a disinfectant."

When Seth was about nine years old, he went out with his grandfather and a cousin. It was out of season, but they went hunting for alligator meat. They came across a big gator, about eleven feet long and heavy, which they got to the boat and shot. To get the big gator in the small boat, they pulled up alongside the alligator near the shore. They grabbed the opposite legs and "rolled" the big lizard into the boat. "That gator was so wide," Seth recalled, "they didn't think its girth would fit in the boat." They balanced the alligator and climbed on board. One of them was smart enough to cover the big gator with a tarp. On top of the tarp, they stuck young Seth and put a fishing rod in his hand. By this time, the game warden had been called to investigate some alligator poachers on the Amite River who had "just killed a big gator." The warden called in a helicopter to help with the search. Meanwhile, Seth, his grandfather, and his cousin slowly motored their way back down river to camp. Along the way, they noticed a helicopter flying up and down the river. The warden in the helicopter looked down and saw a small boat motoring down the river. He looked closer; it was just a few locals fishing and hauling supplies under a tarp, with a small kid sitting on top.

"My uncle was famous for his gumbo," Seth recalled. His gumbo was made with "all the good fixin's—lemon, cayenne peppers, jalapeño peppers, corn on the cob, crawfish, alligator, cypress trout (or bowfin), opossum, and nutria." The nutria is a large semiaquatic rodent. It is actually more closely related to the guinea pig than the South American capybara, for which it is commonly mistaken. Nutria is hunted in the bayou for meat.

When Seth's grandfather passed, the family celebrated his life at Fish Camp. Of course, his uncle made his famous gumbo, which was also being enjoyed by Seth's wife Francesca. Seth knew better than to tell her what the ingredients were, especially the nutria, which he knew could be associated with eating a rodent. Francesca told Seth's uncle she thought the gumbo was delicious and asked him what was in it. Seth grimaced; he knew what was coming. Sure enough, his uncle went right down the list of ingredients. "And what is this white meat that's so tasty?" she asked. His uncle smiled big and said, "Oh baby, that's nutria! That's some good eatin' right thaya." Francesca agreed, but wondered aloud what nutria was. Seth's uncle looked out at the river and pointed. "Well, thaya goes one right about now."

THE CONDICTS OF WYOMING

As I entered my mid-thirties, my hunting world expanded into the American West. The south Georgia hunting club I was a member of with my dad and Mike Owens had a few members who leased access to a ranch in west Texas, near Sheffield, during fall whitetail and spring turkey seasons. I started joining those groups and got my first taste of western open spaces. Those early years in Texas eventually opened the door to other western hunting opportunities, including an invitation to go elk hunting in Wyoming. That was how my dad and I met Mark Condict.

The Condicts embody the spirit of western outfitting. Mark Condict has been guiding and outfitting since he was fifteen years old. His father, Winn Condict III, was among those who pioneered outfitting in Wyoming and, along with fellow outfitter Eddie King, pushed north up into portions of unexplored Alaska. In the fifteen years I have known Mark and his family, we have hunted everything from antelope to mule deer to mountain lion together. Our families have become good friends. I introduced both our son and daughter equally to fishing and hunting at very young ages, and tried to spend time with each of them independently in the field. In fact, my daughter has joined me on most of my hunting and fly fishing trips to Wyoming and is as comfortable on the Condict ranch as anyone. My fascination with tales and stories of seasoned western guides probably began by hanging out with Mark Condict.

One October afternoon, Mark and I were cleaning a mule deer in his barn. Mark pulled out a pair of locked moose antlers from a corner. By locked, I mean two bull moose had been fighting, and their antlers had become permanently locked together in the scrum. This is not uncommon among deer, but it was the first time I had heard of locked antlers with moose. When this occurs in the wild, the two animals typically die. The stronger of the two will break the neck of the weaker; then the stronger, unable to move with the dead weight of the other animal locked to its head, will die of exposure or from predators. Mark's father had spotted the locked moose along a river while flying his single-engine Super Cub. He landed the plane on the riverbank and collected the antlers from the dead animals, which have been locked together ever since. As Mark held the antlers, he began talking about his dad.

"I remember telling my dad one day I couldn't find the horses," Mark told me. "He yelled at me, 'When you find fresh horse shit, you will find the horses!'"

In his day, Mark's dad, Winn Condict, had little patience for excuses. There was too much at stake. If he wasn't hunting elk, bighorn sheep, or tracking mountain lion in Wyoming, he was pushing the boundaries of outfitting far up north in the arctic. Up on the ice of northern Alaska, the engine of his single-engine Super Cub had to be covered to keep it from freezing. If it froze, both he and his hunter could die. He and Eddie King would fly north together, so that if something went wrong, they could rescue each other. There was no Global Rescue back then, no satellite phones to pull from your pack and signal the cavalry to come get you. If the prop didn't turn, you were in deep trouble.

They were hunting giant polar bear, some of the largest seen by white men. Bear with forearms as big around as a man. The biggest bear were far up on the ice, which meant pushing farther and farther north. Once they found a good bear, they would determine which direction it was heading and then position themselves far ahead of the animal and allow it to come to them. Shots were typically close, less than one hundred yards. Winn Condict believed in waiting for the right animal, and the right shot. "He hunted everything with a .270," Mark once told me, even a fifteen-hundred-pound polar bear.

Once the bear was down, it was quickly skinned and brought back to the Super Cub. The polar bear hide added several hundred pounds of weight to the plane. If space became tight in the cabin of the plane, they would strap the hide to the outside struts, like they did farther south with moose antlers. For balance, they strapped something of equal weight of the hide to the opposite strut. They would then drop fuel weight if needed, pray the engine started, go full throttle, and hope they lifted off before hitting a car-sized block of ice.

The only human eyes watching Winn Condict and Eddie King on those adventures were Inuit. Mark continued, "Many had never seen white hunters before. Over time, my dad and Eddie King gained the trust of the local village, and eventually they were invited to go along with the villagers on traditional hunts for walrus, seal, and even whale."

The Condict Ranch is near Saratoga, Wyoming. The ranch has been passed down through the family for generations. The North Platte River runs along the ranch to the west, and the Medicine Bow Mountains tower over the ranch to the east. The game you are pursuing dictates the season you arrive. Early antelope season feels like late summer. The transition to deer season brings veins of bright yellow cottonwood along the riverbeds. I grew up anticipating the autumn red colors of the east coast, but after many years of returning to the Condict ranch each fall to hunt, I look forward to the cottonwood and aspen yellows just as much.

No matter how warm it gets during the day, frost covers each fall morning at the ranch. I grab a hot mug of coffee from the kitchen, walk out to Mark's truck, scrape icy windows, and jump in. My favorite part of a day in the field or on the water is not knowing what I will see that day. Years ago, Mark and I spotted a huge coyote sitting on a hilltop early one morning. As we got closer, we realized it wasn't a coyote; it was an enormous golden eagle standing upright at the very top of the hill, chest feathers reflecting bronze in the morning sun. We had left the house just moments before, and I was already fulfilled for the day. Mark laughed. Like other guides, he appreciates a visitor to his ranch valuing those moments and not just focusing on shooting something. That said, he still fully expected us to find and shoot a nice antelope that day, which we did.

Back at their ranch house, great stories are told around the kitchen table. Even more stories are left untold in the volumes of old hunting photo albums in the basement. I have sat up many nights flipping through the pages of those albums, looking at old photos of Mark and his dad guiding clients to elk, mule deer, mountain lion, and, what would soon become a hunting focus of mine, bighorn sheep.

Many great tales were experienced firsthand at the hunting camps in those old pictures. Of course, Mark has had his share of run-ins with grizzly over the years. A grizzly will hear a gunshot and head toward the sound, hoping to find a carcass. They will even follow the hunters. Mark told me about one night when a big grizzly walked into his hunting camp, right toward him as he sat near the campfire. Mark yelled at the bear, but the grizzly kept coming forward. "It was a big bear," Mark recalled. The bear was not intimidated by Mark's yelling and was advancing right to the edge of the campfire where Mark sat. "That damn bear wouldn't turn around. I kept yelling at it. Finally, I grabbed one of the logs from the campfire and threw it right at the bear." Mark continued to tell me, "The log got stuck in the bear's hide and set the bear's damn back on fire." The next thing Mark knew, the grizzly turned around and ran back into the woods with a flaming rear end. "I could hear that bear groaning as it ran back into the woods and disappeared. That bear didn't bother us again."

On another hunt, Mark and his client had taken an elk up in the high country of Wyoming. They broke camp, packed the elk meat and horses, and had just started the long ride out of the mountains when a grizzly started to follow them. The big bear followed the hunters and horses all the way down the mountains and out to the trailhead, where they had left the horse trailer and pickup. "That bear watched me load the horses onto the trailer," Mark said. "Then the goddamn bear starts walking right up the ramp into the trailer with the horses!" Mark ran around the pickup, jumped in the cab, and pulled the truck forward to knock the bear off the loading ramp. "That damn bear still wouldn't leave!" Mark laughed. But Mark had had enough. He swung the truck around and drove the pickup right into the side of the bear, knocking it down. The big bear finally got the message. It got up and walked off into the woods.

Grizzlies were not the only unwelcome critter to try and walk onto Mark's horse trailer. One year, Mark was hunting elk up in the Wind River Range of western Wyoming. He had a few hunters with him, and they had set up a spike camp far up the valley. The horses were secured and had been given alfalfa for the night. That evening, something came into camp. Instead of clawing at the hanging elk meat, or tearing into the supply tent, the intruder began to steal alfalfa. This occurred every night. Finally, Mark kept watch one night, rifle in hand. It was not long before the thief emerged, and Mark witnessed the attempted robbery. It was a burro, sneaking into the hunting camp and stealing alfalfa. Mark ran the burro off, expecting the trouble would end.

The burro came back. "That time the burro stayed," Mark told me. The burro would come to the edge of the camp, sneak in, grab a piece of alfalfa, and trot off again. This continued the entire hunt. After all the hunters were successful in getting their elk, they broke camp for the ride out. The burro followed them right out of the mountains. Even with Mark and his hunters yelling and throwing rocks at the burro to try and drive it away, it followed them down the trail. At that point, Mark began to give the burro some credit for persistence.

They eventually made it back to the trailhead, with the waiting horse trailer, and began to set up camp. Mark walked over to the empty horse trailer and looked back. Facing him from the forest edge was the burro. Mark then had a change of heart. He walked toward the burro, laid down a handful of alfalfa, and stepped back. The burro hesitated, stepped into the clearing, and ate the alfalfa. Mark took a few steps toward the trailer and did it again. Again, the burro stepped forward and ate the offering. This continued all the way to the trailer, right up the ramp, and then, a few feet at a time, right into the trailer.

The plan was working well until Mark closed the trailer door, and the burro no longer had a handful of alfalfa. At that point, the burro began to destroy the inside of Mark's horse trailer. The only thing that would settle the burro down was another bribe of alfalfa. For several days, Mark bribed that burro to not tear his trailer apart. The routine worked a little better each day until they were ready to leave camp. Mark gathered his horses and prepared to board them on the trailer. The first horses up the ramp were not too pleased to find a burro inside. The burro was not too pleased to share his new home with a bunch of nervous horses.

"There were hooves everywhere, even upside down," Mark said. "That burro climbed on the tack, he climbed on the storage rack—hell, he even climbed on the horses!"

"What did you do?" I asked.

Mark laughed. "I took him home."

That story about the burro leads us to Petey the Mule. A mule is not a burro. A mule is produced when a male burro is crossed with a female horse. Petey was Mark's mule and Mark rode him everywhere. Elk and sheep trails are notoriously dangerous, places where a mule's surefootedness is not only reassuring, it can be a lifesaver. Petey excelled at hauling packs—and Mark—up and down those cliffhanger trails.

Mark's confidence in his mule got the best of him one evening in a local saloon. Mark was standing at the bar, trading stories with several other patrons, when one of the locals questioned Mark's ability to ride his mule. "Damn right I can!" yelled Mark. "Hell, I'll ride that mule right into this bar. I'll spin him around on the dance floor!" Mark turned and quietly walked out of the saloon. A few moments later, the bar doors swung open ... and in rode Mark on Petey the Mule. Mark rode Petey right past the local at the bar, out on to the dance floor. He then spun Petey around a few times, Petey performed flawlessly.

At a moment like this, a story that becomes legend is in the making, but sometimes, moments take unexpected turns. Mark and Petey did not know the bar's wooden dance floor was built over a sunken storage cellar, and while cowboys and cowgirls come in all shapes and sizes, whoever built the dance floor did not anticipate the weight of a dancing mule.

Mark took Petey around for one final spin. He had made his point. The only thing left was for Mark and Petey to take a final bow under the dancing lights and sashay right out the front door of the saloon. Instead, at that very moment, the dance floor gave way, and Mark and Petey dropped straight through the floor, down into the cellar. It took a moment for the dust to settle and for everyone in the saloon to realize what had happened. After an anxious pause in time, Petey re-emerged through the dust, climbing right out of the gaping hole in the floor. And there, still on Petey's back, was Mark. A moment becomes legend.

Of all the great Condict stories, my favorites are probably about the characters Mark came across hunting mountain lion. Mark especially enjoys talking about the old lion hunters, the "Old-Timers." "That generation was different," Mark told me while we were driving in his truck one afternoon. "They don't make them like that anymore." I found Mark's comment ironic, coming from someone else whom they don't make anymore.

"We used to travel from Wyoming down to Nevada to hunt lion," Mark explained. "The guys down there would say they were better lion hunters than us up in Wyoming because they didn't have snow for 'easy tracking.'"

Mark smiled, recalling one old lion hunter he used to work with. "He was a short man with a big hat, and bigger pistol," Mark told me with a grin. "Hell, his pistol was as tall as he was. He would race down those back roads in Nevada, looking for fresh tracks in the dirt, kicking up dust everywhere. As soon as he found tracks, he would slam on the brakes and yell, 'Release the hounds!' That was my cue to let his dogs out the back. I would run around the back of the truck and open the dog crates," Mark recalled. "There would be dogs running everywhere. Each dog would take off in a different direction—except the direction the tracks went."

The old man would jump out of the truck, raise his giant pistol, and start yelling and shooting. "He'd be screaming the whole time, yelling the dogs' names," Mark remembered. Of course, not one of the dogs would listen or come back. "The old man would get so mad, he would start shooting at the dogs, hitting a few ears along the way—it was total chaos," he laughed.

Hunters are passionate, but hunters who work with dogs in the field are fanatical. The relationship between a hunter and their dog is special, to the point of being misunderstood if you have not experienced it yourself. Whether the target of the hunt is upland birds, ducks, raccoon, or mountain lion, there is an unspoken connection between the hunter and their dog. Plain and simple, the hunt is about the dogs; it's not about the hunter or even the game.

Mountain lion hunters are no different. Mark enjoys guiding elk and deer, but is passionate about hunting lion with his dogs. Blue Dog, Red Dog, Yellow Dog—nothing confusing about the names. A few winters ago, I followed Mark on a snowmobile, also called a "snow machine," in the Bighorn Mountains of northern Wyoming. Mark had been brought on by the landowner to help manage the cat population on the ranch where he raised livestock. He was towing Red Dog, Blue Dog, and Yellow Dog in boxes on a sled behind his snowmobile. I was trying to keep up on my own snowmobile, without flipping the thing over.

Mark slowed and pointed to a nasty steep ravine in the distance. "That's the one place we don't want to have to track a lion," he said. I noted the steep ravine, and we continued on. A few inches of snow had fallen the night before, giving us a fresh carpet to look for new tracks. I realized then what Mark had meant a few years prior, when he told me about the challenges of tracking mountain lion in the dirt and dust of Nevada. With our new snowfall, Mark quickly found fresh tracks. We stopped the snowmobiles, and Mark looked closely at the tracks. Once he was satisfied the tracks were left by a cat he wanted to chase, he lifted each dog out of its box, flipped them upside down in his arms, and plunged their noses directly down into the track depression in the snow. The dogs had done this maneuver countless times and inhaled the fresh scent of lion paw. Red Dog, Blue Dog, and Yellow Dog then ran howling up the steep embankment, following the track into the thick spruce. Red Dog and Blue Dog soon turned in one direction.

Yellow Dog ran in another. "Goddamn it, Yellow Dog," Mark muttered. The dogs disappeared, but Mark knew exactly what they were doing and where they were going from their howling and low whooping sounds.

We followed the sound of low howls most of the morning. Red Dog and Blue Dog trailed the mountain lion right into the middle of that horrible ravine Mark had pointed to earlier. The terrain quickly became too steep for the snowmobiles, and we followed on foot. The snow was so deep in places, it covered us up to our armpits. The dogs finally treed the mountain lion halfway up the ravine, and we took it using Mark's old .30-30 lever action Winchester. We packed the lion and our gear and made the long hike back to the snowmobiles, followed by Red Dog and Blue Dog. Yellow Dog was nowhere to be found. "Goddamn it, Yellow Dog!" Mark said under his breath. When we arrived back at the main trail, Mark left Yellow Dog's box on the trail. I asked him why. "The dog will retrace his track back to here," Mark said. "If he finds the box, he will stay in the box until we come back for him; if he doesn't, he will freeze to death." Such is the harsh reality of the Wyoming winter. As we left, I could tell Mark was quietly upset about not finding the dog. The following year, I asked Mark if he ever found Yellow Dog. He did. "Goddamn Yellow Dog."

I once heard a striking comment from an old mountain lion trapper I had come across in southwest Texas. I was hunting mule deer in the Glass Mountains, not far from Marathon, Texas, a place where the sheriff still patrols the more remote sections of his territory on horseback. The mountains along the Mexican border were visible to the south, down by Big Bend National Park. The rugged peaks and ridgelines softened into shades of purple in the distant haze. I remember thinking the mountains looked bigger than I had expected to see in Texas.

I was walking a dirt road with my hunting guide. I had just stopped to help a western diamondback rattlesnake off the road, when an old pickup came rumbling along, kicking up dust. The old man driving stopped to see if we needed help. His old truck was a world of rusty intrigue. The truck was covered in dust and dents and was the general color of west Texas. The dual rear tires, a rarity back home, supported a worn flatbed that may have been painted at one time. What caught my eye were the traps. Large steel jaws, held shut by lengths of chain wrapped tight around each set of springs and teeth. Dozens of them, laying on the steel bed and hanging from a rusted steel rack. Pushed up against the steel mesh protecting the rear window was a heavy steel dog kennel; its sides were also muted rust, blending into the tangled collage of old metal and chain. Two white and black hound muzzles poked out from inside the kennel. Their dark, damp noses, a sharp contrast to the dry dust covering everything, extended out to investigate the sudden stop. Lion hounds. At first glance, they are not much different from the pointers back home, but their eyes told a different story.

Years of odds and ends were tucked into each corner of the truck bed—a screwdriver, a length of chain, an old broken toolbox, and various crushed cans of Mountain Dew and beer. Every bent screw or broken trap coil told a story of a resourceful lion hunter charged with managing the cat population in a remote, rugged valley nowhere near a hardware store and about as far south as one can go in Texas.

The old man noticed my interest in his collection of rusty gear. "You never know what you are going to find in your traps," he said. "The lion move back and forth across those peaks," he noted, pointing south toward the border. "They find the easiest way across those mountains, using the same passes year after year." He hesitated for a minute before continuing. "The lion are not the only ones who use the passes, you know." He looked out over the desert. "It's not unusual to find signs you trapped something with two legs instead of four." The same passes used by generations of mountain lion were also used by generations of people, trying to find their way across the border. "It's easy to tell when you trapped someone sneaking over the mountains," he told me. "There's sign everywhere, trying to free themselves." As he drove off, I couldn't help but think about the significance, and harsh reality, of what he had just said.

The next morning, I was having a cup of coffee in the local café in Marathon. The sheriff walked in and took a seat next to me at the counter. I introduced myself and asked him what it was like having to patrol such a remote area. He told me horseback is the only way to reach many parts of his county. Sometimes he would ride with a deputy or two, sometimes not. "It's not a good feeling riding alone up to a large group of people out in the desert," he said. "They are not usually armed. They carry some food, water, and blankets, but you never know. Those are the moments I don't like."

I finished my coffee and walked out of the café onto the quiet street. I looked south, toward the distant purple mountains of Big Bend; the border beyond, and all the untold stories and secrets hidden forever in those mountain passes.

Base camp in Nunavut was an abandoned arctic research station.

Caribou meat and fat is hung to dry at camp.

RIDR KNOWLTON

*My guide in Nunavut, a respected Inuit tracker,
carries more than his own body weight of
caribou meat on his back.*

RIDR KNOWLTON COLLECTION

*My grandparents, Virginia and Dick Knowlton, Sr.
at the family's fishing camp in the Catskills, near Roscoe,
New York. One of the guests was obviously a bear hunter.
Note the old camp house in the background, where my
grandparents and great-grandparents stayed, and where
my mom, sister, and I stayed while my dad was in Vietnam.*

My father, Dick Knowlton, Jr.,
along Ebenezer Creek near Savannah, Georgia.

RIDR KNOWLTON

The swamps of the Savannah River.

RIDR KNOWLTON

Steele Hawkins with a Georgia gobbler.

*The Cricket II on the docks at Captain's Cove Marina,
Montauk, NY (early '80s).*

Seth Vernon heading out on his flats boat.

RIDR KNOWLTON

Mark Condict and I up in the Bighorns of Wyoming. Note Mark's lion hounds off to the side and the old .30-30 lever action rifle, complete with a shoelace sling.

MARK AND VALERIE CONDICT

Mark Condict's father, Winn Condict III, at sixteen years old with an outstanding mule deer from the Wyoming family ranch in 1941.

Mark Condict packing out an elk in the Bighorn Mountains of Wyoming.

Mike McCann with an impressive dall ram.

On a scouting traverse of 8,000-foot,
snow-covered peaks in southern British Columbia.

RIDR KNOWLTON

Tack and gear at base camp in the Brooks Range of northern Alaska.

RIDR KNOWLTON

*Spike camp during an early season blizzard in the Brooks Range of Alaska.
The creek to the right froze every night.*

A big grizzly print I came across in southwestern Alaska.
A reminder you are no longer the top of the food chain.

Glassing sheep country in the
Cassiar Mountains of northern British Columbia.

This was a welcome sight back at spike camp in the Cassiars. First hot meal in several days consisted of sheep back straps, a few remaining eggs, and hot coffee brewed in an old paint can over the open fire.

A classic meal of the high country, sheep ribs, barbequed over an open fire back at base camp. This was my dall ram, taken earlier that same day, in the Brooks Range.

*Homer Rhode with a fine snook.
Note the fly rod in his right hand.*

*Dead bird-eating spider from
South America. Note hand
used for size reference.*

RIDR KNOWLTON

*Our kids found a scorpion near our cabin on the Osa Peninsula of Costa Rica.
We released it back into the jungle after the photo was taken.*

RIDR KNOWLTON

*Small puff adder found roadside in the Matetsi area of NW Zimbabwe.
Note the skin pattern, a highly effective camouflage.*

Bill (kneeling), Linda (right), and Corie Fuchs (left) with the massive man-eating crocodile Bill hunted on the Kilombero River in Tanzania.

Helping a western diamondback
off a dirt road in southwest Texas.

Bill Fuchs' childhood friend, Bobby
Leach, with the huge diamondback
rattlesnake they found near the
Everglades. The snake measured seven
feet four inches in length.

MOUNTAIN GUIDES

Many of the most experienced and hardcore guides I know are sheep or "mountain" hunters. This includes, of course, the Condicts, who have guided rocky mountain bighorn sheep hunts for generations and are considered one of America's legendary sheep hunting families.

My own desire to climb mountains and pursue the great rams of North America was surely inspired by the Condicts, but was probably born from an unexpected hunting experience where I, really for the first time, learned firsthand the importance of physically preparing for a trip.

I was part of a small group hunting mule deer in southwest Texas. One morning I was out with one of the younger guides and another hunter. A buddy of mine was guiding a different group in the same area when he spotted a huge band of aoudad sheep, high in a bowl between two mountains, not far from our location. He called us on the radio and said he thought there might be some big rams in the group and that we should go take a look.

Aoudad sheep are not indigenous to North America. They were introduced from North Africa and now thrive in the desert mountains of Texas. They are a large, impressive animal with sweeping horns and a long mane of hair. I had never seen an aoudad, or even been interested in hunting sheep, but we started climbing. The other hunter with us was a nice guy from Ohio, but he was overweight and out of shape. Halfway up the front slope of the first mountain, he was visibly struggling. The young guide and I both became increasingly concerned about his condition and safety and eventually made the decision to turn around. The two of us got him safely off the mountain and back to our vehicle, where there was shelter, plenty of water, and a radio.

The guide and I then turned around and started climbing again. Hours later, as we crested the front ridge, it began snowing and I looked across the deep bowl, getting my first glimpse of a big ram. I will never forget the image of that desert ram in the snow, but the real inspiration to become a sheep hunter had occurred a few hours before, as I was helping that other hunter down the mountain. For the first time as a sportsman, I realized some places in the wild would only be accessible to those who were properly prepared, and that the preparation, both physical and mental, was all part of the hunt.

One of my sporting and business mentors from Atlanta, John Heagy, is an accomplished mountain climber and sportsman. He has summited significant peaks in the Andes and Alps as well as glacial mountains in the Pacific Northwest. His son, Anderson, was a climbing guide on Mt. Rainier for years. John's training regimen before a big climb included carrying a weighted backpack up and down the stairwells of some of Atlanta's tallest office buildings. This technique intrigued me because it built strength and endurance, but also balance, from lugging a weighted pack. An additional benefit of this type of training is that you can break in your climbing boots prior to the actual climb, arguably the most important preparation of all. I learned from John's regimen and applied it to my own preparation for mountain hunting, again trying to capture natural balance. I started with training climbs on lesser mountains with a weighted pack, but eventually I added a simple step—a rock, usually about ten or fifteen pounds.

My rock rule was simple: I could carry the rock any way I wanted, on ascent and descent, but I could not put it down until arriving back at the trailhead. Theoretically, the awkwardness created by the rock required subtle muscle use, which I thought might help me manage a rifle or animal's hindquarter more effectively in the field. One year, I found a particularly perfect rock of just the right weight and shape. I even found myself trying to hide the rock after a climb so it would not to be noticed by another hiker and picked up. As it turned out, I was the only one interested in carrying the rock, and it lay unmolested near a trailhead in western North Carolina for years, where I imagine it still lies today.

There are four indigenous species of North American sheep. Two of the four are considered "bighorns" and two are considered "thinhorns." The bighorn rams include the iconic rocky mountain bighorn, which is found along the Rocky Mountains of the American and Canadian west, and the desert bighorn sheep of the southwestern US and Mexico. As you would expect, the two thinhorn rams have more narrow horns than their bighorn cousins. The thinhorns live in the far north and include the majestic snow white dall sheep of Alaska, Canada's Northwest Territories, northwest British Columbia, and the Yukon, and the elusive, beautiful stone sheep found in northern British Columbia and the Yukon. Successfully hunting any of the rams is incredibly challenging and a highlight of any hunting career. For some, who get the "sheep bug" like I did, they make a life goal of trying to hunt all four. Along the way, I met guides who became valued friends and introduced me to a whole new level of wilderness. In this chapter, I share some of the stories from the northern guides with whom I pursued the thinhorned rams.

Following that aoudad sheep hunt in Texas, I immersed myself in the world of North American sheep hunting. There are many challenges in organizing a sheep hunt, even before getting to the mountains, including accessing hard to find hunting permits, or "tags" as they are called, the logistics of a mountain hunt, and the cost. Sheep hunts are among the most expensive hunts in the world. I quickly realized the only way I could afford sheep hunting would be to follow outfitters closely and wait for last-minute "canceled" hunts. When this happens, a hunter, who may have paid sizeable upfront deposits, is not able to go on the trip, and the outfitter, who is now trying to fill the spot last minute, can offer a significant discount to another hunter if they can join the trip with little notice. For someone like me, who was relying on those discounted rates, it meant if I was going to experience sheep hunting, I would have to be patient and take opportunities as they came. I luckily met experienced sheep hunters along the way who helped me navigate the strategies of pursuing permits and outfitters, including Rex Baker, a neighbor of mine back in Atlanta. Meeting Rex was fortuitous to say the least. Rex is one of the most accomplished hunters in the world and widely regarded as one of the world's leading sheep hunters. When I first met Rex, I did not realize who he was, let alone his endless accomplishments. However, once Rex learned about my fledgling interest in sheep hunting, he offered sage advice and early inspiration.

It turned out the first "canceled hunt" I was offered was for a stone sheep, considered by many to be the most challenging of the four due to the very remote and rugged locations of their habitat. I was as inexperienced and green a sheep hunter as it gets, and jumped right in the deep end. Having now successfully hunted all four rams, I look back and am thankful I started with the stone. I faced every imaginable challenge on that first trip, which I know prepared me for the next three sheep.

No matter how hard you train before an adventure, the wilderness quickly finds weakness. Soon after meeting my stone sheep guide at our base camp in northern British Columbia, we began packing for the following day's ride up to a spike camp high in the mountains. As we were packing food rations, he told me a story about a call he had once received from a sports manager of a top international triathlete.

The triathlete asked his manager to find the most challenging adventure he could do anywhere in the world. After researching various ultra-marathons and off-road races around the world, the manager concluded that due to the physical requirements, inhospitable remote locations, and objective to pursue a wary animal that thrives on exposed mountains and cliffs, the most challenging adventure you can do is a stone sheep hunt. He informed the athlete, who immediately booked a hunt with my guide.

As we continued to pack supplies for our own hunt, he smiled as he told me about the small plane that began making supply airdrops, at the same base camp I was staying, of special nutrition and protein foods prior to the arrival of the athlete. This went on for over a week. Finally, the athlete arrived at base camp. The following morning, they packed the horses and left base camp to start climbing. The triathlete lasted less than three hours. It wasn't the physical challenge; it was the relentless beating he took from heavy, broken branches as the packhorses pushed through the dense underbrush on the lower flanks of the mountain. The triathlete called it quits. They returned to base camp, and he flew home the next day.

I should qualify that I am not a seasoned athlete. I am your typical, out-of-shape workaholic who spends an unhealthy amount of time sitting in an office. I am just as likely to be twenty-five pounds overweight from a steady diet of late-night Breyers mint chip as I am to be training for a mountain hunt. We climbed for thirteen hours my first day on the stone sheep hunt. I began vomiting around the second hour.

My hunt took place in the Cassiar Mountains (pronounced Kazziar). The Cassiars are the northern most interior range of British Columbia. They are some of the most remote and rugged mountains I have hunted or explored. The best access to the Cassiars is by bush plane, typically from Fort Ware, an aboriginal community of about three hundred, located near the confluence of the Finlay, Kwadacha, and Fox Rivers that flow together in the bowels of the Rocky Mountain Trench. The "Trench," as it is called, is a deep valley that runs along the western side of the Rocky Mountains from Montana up toward the Yukon, eventually separating the northern Canadian Rocky Mountains in the east from the Cassiar Mountains to the west.

Access to Fort Ware is limited to bush plane or driving to the end of a sixty-kilometer logging road. From the village, you can continue north on horse trails, up through the Rocky Mountain Trench, eventually reaching the Alaskan Highway. The ride is said to take about two weeks. The village has a gravel runway, community buildings, and scattered gatherings of small homes along narrow dirt roads. There are random trucks, but most in the village drive snow machines or, in the brief months of summer, ATVs. Like any community in the far north, the village is set up for winter year-round. Streets, vehicles, and yard equipment can look scattered and disheveled to a summertime visitor. However, everything is right where it is supposed to be; it's just missing three feet of snow.

For a northern sheep hunter pursuing the thinhorned rams of Alaska and northern Canada, the choices of hunting seasons are either mosquito season or snow season. Mosquito season, or July, offers the best chance at good weather and early looks at rams. Snow season, or late August and September, offers questionable weather, but no mosquitos and, if you are so inclined, the ability to also hunt moose and bear. Being focused on sheep, I opted for the mosquitos in the Cassiars. They did not disappoint.

Our spike camp was high on the western edge of the Rocky Mountain Trench. For several days, we were fogged in and exposed to severe lightning storms, one of which ignited a forest fire in the valley below us. The fire grew, bellowing dense smoke right up the ridgeline to our camp. The smoke got so thick, we couldn't see anything. It was worse than the fog. The conditions made glassing for sheep impossible, so we hunkered down and began rationing food. We did this for several days, a handful of granola in the morning and a few slices of cheese or moose sausage at night. Finally, another storm came through, which knocked out the fire and cleared the skies, allowing us to glass for sheep the following morning. We quickly found two good rams a mile away high on a rocky outcrop overlooking the valley floor. The stalk was unforgettable, culminating in a long traverse along a narrow sheep trail nine hundred feet up a steep shale edge. We were rewarded with a twenty-five-yard shot, one of the closer stalks on a stone sheep I have heard of. The ram tumbled from the ledge and hung up on a small boulder just below us, a ridiculous offering of good fortune.

We had our ram but, more importantly, we had meat. We butchered the sheep right on the small boulder. There was no need to poke our heads up squirrel-like every thirty seconds to look for bear. We were all alone up high on that steep shale slope. Our biggest concern was keeping our balance on the loose rock while we packed meat, horns, and cape into our packs. Not an ounce of meat was wasted. We climbed down off the mountain and, several hours later, as the last gray light dimmed, we trudged into spike camp. It was probably close to midnight. We grabbed the first slab of meat from the top of my pack, filleted it into medallions, added salt, and threw them on an iron skillet heating over the campfire along with a few eggs we had carefully packed in the depths of the panniers, or sidebags, for a special occasion. It was a beautiful sight. We used an old paint can to brew coffee in the fire and devoured the sizzling skillet of meat. We repeated this process for much of the night. Grab the next hunk of meat from the pack ... slice it up ... add salt ... throw on the skillet ... eat in silence ... repeat. Like gorging lions, our appetites were insatiable.

After securing our stone ram, and devouring it on the mountainside, we moved further west to the interior of the Cassiars, where the mountains became higher, jagged, and more unforgiving, to look for mountain goat. It's been said the only thing tougher than a sheep hunt is a goat hunt. I have found this to be true.

Similar to the sheep hunt, we packed light with minimal provisions. Fog covered our spike camp early and cleared by mid-morning. The snow-white goats were easy to spot against the distant black rock above the tree line. We glassed several, including an old mature billy high on exposed rock, thousands of feet above our camp. Our climb from camp to goat took most of the day, resulted in a forty-five-degree-angled uphill shot that luckily dropped the billy just twenty-five feet from a thousand-foot abyss. If the goat had rolled just one or two more times, we never would have recovered the animal. A mountain goat is a surprisingly big critter under the thick white coat. A mature male can weigh over two hundred fifty pounds. My guide and I split the harvested meat equally between our two packs and quickly began the descent, which was far more difficult and dangerous than the climb up. Our line off the mountain was nearly vertical in places with the only purchase on the exposed rock face being young spruce roots grasping to random crevices, which allowed an exposed peg-board style descent with our heavy, meat-filled packs.

We stumbled into spike camp late that night and ate the last of our Mountain House, freeze-dried food, determined to return to Fort Ware a few days later with plenty of goat meat to share with the village. Sure enough, a few days later, we did make it back to Fort Ware, where we were invited, along with our goat, to join the village chief and his family for dinner. It was an honor to be invited to their home. I knew I was only included because of the relationship my guide had with the chief, but the entire family welcomed me warmly. Their house was a welcome respite from the cold, wet spike camps we had been calling home. Dinner was white rice and mountain goat. It was outstanding.

After dinner, I sat with the chief in his living room. We spoke about the hunt and the wilderness surrounding Fort Ware. Eventually, discussion turned to the village. After a while, I looked at him and asked sincerely, "Do you like being chief?" He looked away and thought about it for less time than I would have expected. "No, I don't like being chief," he answered. I asked him why and will never forget what he said. A slight dejected look came to his face. "I have been chief for three years. In those years, we have lost nearly a quarter of the village population of young men to alcohol-related violent deaths. They get drunk and fight. If they don't shoot or stab each other, they take their snow machines out on the river at night and get killed on the ice."

I didn't really know how to respond. I was staggered by what he had just said. I thought about the numerous Inuit villages in both Canada and Alaska where I had spent time, and the warm and wonderful people I had met in those villages. I knew they all faced that same terrible challenge with alcohol, and they all had leaders who felt helpless at times. The moment passed, and I sat with the chief for another few hours, appreciating his warm home, listening to stories, and just enjoying the feeling of a full stomach.

* * *

Alaska is home to several mountain ranges, each with different features and personalities. For the sheep hunter, the classic ranges are the Alaska Range, the coastal Chugach, the Wrangell Mountains, and the northern Brooks Range.

The long and narrow Alaska Range horseshoes from the eastern border with the Yukon, up and around Anchorage and Denali, then down toward the Aleutians. Due to its proximity to Anchorage and Denali National Park, the Alaska Range is probably the most recognized and traveled of the four. One of Alaska's premier sheep hunting areas is the Tok Management Area (TMA) in the eastern Alaskan Range. To many, the TMA permit is the ultimate Alaskan sheep tag, much like drawing the Missouri Breaks bighorn tag in the lower forty-eight.

Southeast of Anchorage, the rugged, glacial Chugach Mountains command impressive prominence originating at sea level and piling upon each other to coastal elevations above 11,000 feet. Because of their proximity to the coastal moisture of Prince William Sound and the Gulf of Alaska, the Chugach have one of the highest annual rain and snowfall levels on earth, with certain areas receiving over fifty feet of snow per year. Conditions in the Chugach can be severe, but for those willing to take on the challenge, they have some of the largest dall sheep on earth.

North and east of the Chugach, the Wrangell Mountains are big, rugged, and steep with overhanging glaciers. The Wrangells, along with parts of British Columbia, are some of the most dramatically scenic places to hunt in North America. During the winter months, long after the sheep hunters have left, the interior of the Wrangells, blocked from warmer currents coming off the seawater by the Chugach, can become one of the coldest places on Earth.

Finally, to the far north, above the Arctic Circle, lies the Brooks Range. Running the width of Alaska from the Yukon to the Chukchi Sea, just below the North Slope oil fields, the Brooks can be deceiving. In summer, photos of the Brooks can look downright warm and inviting, with sloping mountains covered in blueberry bushes beginning to redden with the approaching cooler autumn temperatures. Don't be fooled. The Brooks are one of the most remote and uninhabited places in North America. They are North America's northernmost divide, distributing drainage flows between the northern Pacific and Arctic Oceans. I met Mike McCann when he was living and trapping in the Wrangells and guiding in the Brooks. Like my stone sheep hunt, Mike had a sheep hunter who canceled last minute, providing me a tremendous opportunity to pursue both dall sheep and grizzly bear in the fabled Brooks Range.

Mike is now an outfitting consultant and writer, but prior to that, Mike guided in Alaska for over forty years, leading clients to brown bear on the peninsula, caribou and bear out of Nome, sheep in the Chugach and Wrangles, and for over twenty years, sheep, bear, and moose up north in the Brooks. If you picture the classic rugged "Grizzly Adams" image of an Alaskan trapper and guide, it looks like Mike McCann. Mike is as hard and tough as they get, but his eyes light up with interest in the world around him. I think that's why our friendship continues, as observers, documenting the outdoors. I consider myself lucky to have spent time sitting around Mike's campfires in a legendary place like the Brooks, listening to incredible stories of a cold, unforgiving place, looking into the flames for warmth with the strange green northern lights radiating overhead.

One of my fly fishing buddies from Atlanta is a well-read basketball player from Davidson College named Dick Myrick. In addition to "knocking the shoulders off" a gallon jug of bourbon better than anyone I know, twenty-five years ago, Dick began the long-standing tradition among our fly fishing group of recounting Robert Service's poem, "The Cremation of Sam McGee," around our campfire at night. That poem captures the cold of the northern woods like no other, and, to this day, every time I hear those frozen words, I think of those nights in the Brooks Range.

Mike could not personally guide me on my hunt because, a few months earlier, his leg had gotten stuck in the track of his snow machine. The track had grabbed and pulled his leg into the machine, only stopping when his leg muscle and bone became so imbedded in the gears that friction allowed no more movement. Luckily, this occurred at Mike's home and his son came running to his screams. Finding his severely injured dad, he immediately shut off the snow machine and went to find help. Mike was then quickly rushed to medical aid.

Mike was sincere when he told me how lucky he was that the snow machine accident occurred at his home, where rescue was possible. It easily could have occurred out in the bush, on his trap line in the Wrangell Mountains, where he could have been the only person for twenty miles and temperatures can plummet to fifty below. Mike told me, very matter-of-fact, "If the accident happened while I was trapping, I would have frozen to death that evening and been eaten by wolves the next day." We were both thinking the same unspoken truth, which was that he would have been "lucky" if he froze to death first ... before the wolves found him.

I experienced many of the "classic" sheep hunting challenges pursuing my stone ram in the Cassiars, including being fogged in, smoked in, stranded on exposed rock in lightning storms, and all the painful bonding moments you share with your horse while climbing and descending below the tree line. The one box I had yet to check was hypothermia, which the Brooks Range was happy to provide.

The process of even getting to the Brooks Range is an adventure in itself. From Fairbanks, Alaska, I flew north to an outpost village located about thirty-five miles above the Arctic Circle called "Bettles." Bettles is only accessible by bush plane or, during the winter months, snow machine. As of the 2010 census, Bettles had a population of twelve people.[2] Bettles is a neat town, and one I hope to return to, with a small but efficient airstrip, park office for the Gates of the Arctic National Park, and warm, welcoming lodge with a fireplace and kitchen. Bettles is a primary take-off location for those heading up to the Brooks Range, but is even more famous for being a world-renowned location to photograph the northern lights, or aurora borealis. There were a handful of outdoor photographers from around the world staying at the lodge while I was there, and it was fascinating watching them prepare their equipment for the evening show of dazzling green and sometimes white or reddish lights. I am fortunate to have seen the northern lights dozens of times throughout the arctic, but I have only ever seen the green lights.

From Bettles I took a four-seat bush plane, with two other hunters, north into the Brooks Range. An hour prior to loading our gear onto the small plane, I noticed the peaks of the Brooks, barely visible in the distance to the north, had received snow the night before. It was late July and, even in northern Alaska where July snow flurries are not uncommon, my gut told me it was a sign of poor weather to come. I was right.

We left the flat terrain around Bettles, and the small plane increased elevation as we entered the mountains. I never get tired of seeing the mountains from a small bush plane. The bush pilots are some of the best in the world, and you feel like you can reach out and grab the exposed rock as you wisp by the mountain edges, just meters away. The pilot landed on the banks of a river far within the range, where a line of pack horses and a few of Mike's guides were waiting to meet us. From the river, it was another forty-five-minute ride to base camp, where I first met Mike.

We all settled into camp, preparing to head out the next day. Each of us would ride out with our guide up different valley drainages, looking for sheep. My guide was a great fellow from New Zealand named Kemble, and we left base camp in good weather and spirits, heading up a valley to the north. Within a few hours, light flurries began to appear. An hour later, we emerged from the tree line and Kemble spotted a grizzly across a steep ravine and river. If we wanted a shot at the bear, we would need to ford the icy river on foot as it was too steep and unsafe for the horses. Normally, this would not be a big deal but, given the worsening weather, we considered the implications of soaking our boots and clothing, especially since we were trying to avoid campfires as the slightest whiff of smoke can push grizzly out of a valley. We decided to go for it and crossed the deep, icy rapids. We reached the far side and began crawling up the steep slope on all fours, through gripping alders and berry bushes, trying to get above the bear. Unfortunately, the bear, who had not smelled us yet, also decided to climb higher and angle toward us. Suddenly, I looked up from my crouch. Twenty yards away stood the grizzly. He stood upright looking at me for a few brief moments, before dropping back to all fours, turning, and crashing away through the brush. The bear was gone, and we were soaked.

The climb back down the mountainside was silent, as both of us reconsidered our decision and current situation. We were completely soaked through, the snow was now blowing hard, the temperature had dropped forty degrees, and if we were going to remain committed to hunting grizzly as well as sheep, we knew spike camp would offer no comfort from fire. We reloaded the horses and pushed onward in silence into the storm, which got worse and worse. Finally, we found a small stream and, out of necessity, hurriedly set up two tents and a lean-to to cover the saddles. The temperature continued to drop. The inside of my tent was quickly dusted with snow brought in on wet clothes and gear. That same snow would remain unmelted inside my tent for the next several days.

We made the most of the conditions. We had plenty of supplies, and while the nearby creek froze each night, we could break and melt ice for water. The cold, however, was unforgiving. The skies cleared at night, dropping temperatures even further. We learned to sleep with our boots in the sleeping bags, as they would otherwise harden into icy blocks, with stiff laces sticking out like frozen, jagged bolts of electricity.

We spent the next three days hoping for a break in the weather. The second afternoon, Kemble and I made an attempt to climb higher in elevation and cross over into the next valley in the hope of finding a safer place for the horses, which had not eaten since the storm. It was impassable. As we increased elevation, three or four feet of snow covered a fragile layer of ice, below which sat another foot or more of spongy wet tundra. The horses would not be able to make it safely across that terrain. As we pushed to the top of the pass, a wave of nausea and uncontrollable shaking hit me, both of which I caused. The nausea was a result of poor hydration as we climbed. The chills came on from not properly managing my clothing layers between climbing and resting. In any event, those two mistakes resulted in a mild case of hypothermia up on the pass. I started vomiting and shaking uncontrollably. Kemble had to lead me back down the mountain to our spike camp where he helped me into my bag and quickly melted ice for a hot drink. The shaking subsided as we got hot fluids into me, and I was good to go a few hours later. The reality is I experienced a "tame" reminder of the danger of not being respectful of the Alaskan wilderness. Those same mistakes, alone in the Alaskan winter, mean you don't come home.

On the fourth day, the weather turned for the better and we broke spike camp, leading our famished horses back down to base camp to resupply. The storm had blown over, and conditions were improving, as were our spirits. The thick canvas-walled tents of base camp were a luxury, and the camp stoves brought warmth we had not felt in days. I asked Mike, who had been managing base camp during the storm, what the temperature had fallen to. "Ten degrees," he said. If it was ten degrees in the warmth and shelter of the valley floor, I can't imagine what the temperature had been up on the exposed mountainsides of our little spike camp.

Over the next three days, we gathered new horses and had epic hunting. I secured a fine full curl dall ram, the last of the sheep I needed to complete my "Grand Slam" of the four North American sheep. We also rode south of base camp, where Kemble and I crawled over a mile to within thirty yards of a massive interior grizzly bear, taking what would be one of the largest grizzly from the Brooks Range in nearly ten years.

Once we had the sheep and bear back at base camp, I had time to start sharing stories with Mike. One afternoon, we were talking about wolverine, the largest member of the weasel family and known for its fearless and ferocious behavior. A wolverine had snuck into our camp the night before and hauled off the sheep horns and hide belonging to one of the other hunters. Luckily, there was fresh snow, making it easy to follow the wolverine's tracks as he dragged away the heavy horns. About seventy-five yards into the brush, one of the other guides found the horns and what remained of the pelt. The metal tag required by Alaska Fish and Game had been chewed on, but it was still intact and clipped to the cape. Can you imagine having to tell Fish and Game that a wolverine ate your sheep tag? The hunter was happy to have recovered his horns. A dall sheep cape is easily replaced, and the hunter got to go home with a good story.

"I once saw a wolverine fight off a grizzly from a kill," Mike told me. "Is there anything more ferocious than a wolverine?" I asked, knowing Mike had run trap lines in the Wrangell Mountains for decades. "No," he said. "Wolverine are not like lynx. Lynx die when trapped. Trapped wolverine are never dead when you find them—they are just pissed off."

This fact was reinforced one morning as Mike was checking his trap line back in the Wrangell Mountains. He realized he had forgotten his .22-caliber rifle as he walked up on a very large, angry wolverine in one of his traps. Mike thought about the situation. The wolverine thought about ripping apart the first piece of Mike that got too close. The only thing Mike had handy was an extra lynx snare, basically a small wire lasso. Mike lassoed the wolverine around the neck and pulled the snare as hard as he could, attempting to strangle it. Instead of getting strangled, the wolverine just became more enraged and began pulling against Mike with equal force. The tug-of-war battle continued until the wolverine pulled himself right out of the leg trap. Mike now had an enraged wolverine on a leash, which somehow ended up between his legs. Desperate, Mike took advantage of his size, grabbed an ax that was lying a few feet away, and dispatched the big weasel with the handle of the ax before it did any permanent damage.

Years later, Mike found himself in a similar situation without his .22. Mike had asked to borrow a .22 from a friend, who agreed and packed the gun in Mike's gear. As Mike approached one of the traps, he found himself face-to-face with yet another highly irritated wolverine. Mike reached into his pack expecting to pull out his friend's standard .22-caliber pistol. What came out instead was a belt buckle, which held a miniature snub nose .22. The pistol was so small, it fit into the belt buckle. Not only was the weapon seriously undersized, it held only four bullets. Of course, with a barrel barely over an inch long, every bullet would be going in a different direction. "I took four shots at that wolverine and all four missed," Mike recalled. Four shots, four misses, one furious wolverine, and one trapper who was tired of the whole damn thing. Mike ended up using his ax, once again.

Mike built his trapper's cabin in the Wrangells by hand, with timber he felled. The cabin has no windows, which makes it easier to insulate and keep the bears out. Mike's closest neighbor is thirty miles away. "That old man was a real survival guy, living off the land, not wasting anything," Mike told me. "Every once in a while, he would go to Fairbanks and come back with a bunch of frozen chickens. He would cook the chickens in a broth and then pull the meat from the bones. The bones would then be placed in a tin jar on the shelf. When he ran out of chicken meat, he would reboil the bones and chew and swallow them," Mike recalled. "He would eat every bone, eat them all."

According to Mike, one of the worst tasting meats in the Alaskan bush is martin. A martin is a small weasel, a smaller, much less ferocious cousin of the wolverine. "Nothing tastes worse than martin," Mike told me. One day, Mike checked his traps and snared a martin. Mike took the martin back to his camp and began to skin it for the hide. The old man was visiting and asked Mike, "What are you going to do with that martin meat? I'll take it if you don't want it." Mike wanted no part of the weasel and handed the thread of meat to the old man, who looked like he had just won the jackpot. The old man started walking away in the snow and looked back at Mike, inviting him over for a few games of cards that evening. "Sure, why not?" Mike replied. Coming over for cards, during the icy months of trapping season, is not a simple commitment, but Mike wanted to be neighborly and accepted the invitation. Mike showed up for cards. The old man had the table ready, along with a pot of warm stew for dinner. "Help yourself to stew," he said. "What kind of stew are we having?" Mike asked, lifting the top off the pot for a better smell. "Martin," the old man replied.

* * *

A guide's experience gives them a different perspective of danger than their hunter. I find hunters, or clients, think about the dangers of things they are not used to being around, such as dangerous animals and game, possibly riding a horse over rough terrain, or, of course, in warmer climates, the ever-present concern of venomous snakes. Guides, on the other hand, seem to focus on those things in the field that they do not control, like unpredictable weather or an overly excited hunter.

I asked Mike one time what he worried about most during the long trapping and hunting seasons in Alaska. I assumed he would talk about wolves, grizzly, an angry bull moose, or even herds of caribou or musk ox, which have, in the past, trampled through his camps from time to time.

Actually, the year before I met Mike, his wife and infant son had joined him at his camp in the Brooks Range. Their plan was to stay until the weather began to worsen, when the moose hunters arrived. Late one night, Mike heard strange noises outside their tent. He thought it could be a bear or wolf, trying to get into one of the tents. Mike had once shot a black bear at point-blank range that walked right into his tent and up to his cot while he was sleeping. He did not want a repeat of that encounter with his wife and child next to him. Mike instinctively grabbed his loaded .44 pistol in one hand, his infant son in the other, and pushed open the loose canvas opening of his tent, looking out into the dark cold for the hump of a grizzly or flash of a wolf. He saw something big by the storage shed. Mike looked closer. Staring back at Mike was a bull musk ox. The wooly creature proceeded to trample through camp, including rummaging through the supply tent before Mike was able to drive the shaggy beast away. Once he was sure the musk ox had left for good, he returned to his tent. His wife was still under the covers in the cot and asked him what the trouble was. Mike responded quietly, "Oh, nothing," as he placed his infant son back in the cot and his .44 back in its holster. "It was nothing, go back to sleep."

Instead of all those dangers I figured Mike would mention, what he talked about were river crossings and icy roads. The most important factor affecting Mike's ability to cover his trap lines in the Wrangell Mountains is snow cover and ice conditions. Snow cover dictates how far, and where, you can travel on your snowmobile. Ice conditions dictate which rivers you can cross, and where. If the river is frozen solid, you can cross. If it isn't, you may well lose your life by trying to do so. During the particular year we were discussing this, the Wrangells were facing an early thaw and Mike was concerned about certain river crossings he would need to make. In the end, it was too dangerous. He decided to let the trap line rest that year.

With all the inherent dangers of managing a hunting camp in the remote Brooks Range, it was the road conditions the first few miles of the Dalton Highway, as Mike begins his long drive home at the end of the season, that worried him the most. The Dalton Highway was built in the early 1970s as a supply road to support the Trans-Alaska Pipeline System. It runs over four hundred miles north from just outside of Fairbanks to Deadhorse, Alaska, on the Arctic Ocean. It is one of the most isolated roads in the United States, and travelers are widely encouraged to carry survival gear. Of the four hundred rugged miles, the highest elevations occur in the Brooks Range.

After the hunting season ends, Mike and his crew break camp and begin the long ride out of the mountains. When they eventually arrive at the Dalton, the horses, gear, and tack are loaded on a trailer, which they leave on the side of the road at the beginning of the season. Mike's trailer would haul six or eight horses. That's a lot of weight, especially being pulled by an average-sized pickup truck. At the beginning of the season, road conditions are not typically an issue. However, at the end of the fall moose season, when early winter ice storms hit the Brooks, the steeper grades on the Dalton Highway coming south out of the mountains can be a death trap for those with overbearing loads.

"Sometimes, you just hold on tight and ride it out," Mike told me. "Other times, when the road gets really icy, it's not worth taking the risk." On those days, Mike would unpack all the horses and gear and make camp right on the side of the Dalton, waiting for that one mile of road to thaw. Sometimes it would take an afternoon, sometimes a week.

THE FUCHS

As noted earlier in the book, we raised our family in the quickly growing suburbs of Atlanta. One of our "escapes" was a small cabin we bought in the mountains of western North Carolina. The cabin was only two hours—but a world—away and we spent every weekend we could there. The cabin was a mountain refuge to my family, but offered me something else entirely—new untapped wall space for antlers. My wife has always supported my hunting and fishing and has even given the thumbs-up to a surprising number of antlers hanging in our house. But the cabin offered expansive, new "real estate" for hanging horns, all disguised under the premise that it was "needed for rustic cabin ambiance." It was one of my few brilliant moves.

Once I secured the wall space, I needed a good taxidermist to help me fill it up. One afternoon, I decided to explore the back roads that wound from our property over various mountain passes. As I explored to the northwest, I crossed over one of the higher passes in the area and down a deep valley toward Franklin, North Carolina. While driving along, I came upon a large barn located near the side of the road. The barn had an impressive elk statue out front. But what caught my eye and caused me to stop was that in the window of the barn was a full body mount of a bongo. Now, for those readers who are not familiar with hunting the spiral-horned antelope of Africa, I completely understand you may have no idea what a bongo is. A bongo is a big-bodied antelope with long spiraled horns and, believe it or not, is rusty orange in color with vertical white stripes. In the hunting world, there are few achievements more highly regarded than successfully pursuing the elusive bongo in the steaming, thick jungles of Central Africa. I obviously had to stop and knock on the door.

When you meet Bill Fuchs, you are greeted with a smile and an iron grip. You may notice his left hand is missing two fingers, which were blown off when he was young while spear fishing in Florida with his brother. They were diving with bang sticks, a short rod with a live shotgun shell at one end that, when stabbed into the side of a fish, will discharge. While Bill was loading his stick, the sixteen-gauge shell exploded, blowing off a sizeable portion of his left hand. The nature of Bill's accident is a reflection of his remarkable life.

Bill is a good friend, and one of the most interesting people I have ever met. Before becoming a world-renowned taxidermist, Bill spent his childhood following his father through the jungles of Central and South America, searching for new species of orchids, which they sold from their family home site in the wilds of south Florida.

THE EVERGLADES

Bill's grandfather, Fred Fuchs, Sr., was born to a German immigrant named Charles T. Fuchs, who settled his family in the Everglades in the late 1800s. The Everglades of south Florida are thick and endless. Before the Glades were dissected by canals and "tamed" by man, the vast river flowed slowly south for a hundred miles, from Lake Okeechobee to Biscayne and the Florida Bays. It ran sixty miles wide and six inches deep, fed by Lake Okeechobee and south Florida's fifty inches of annual rainfall. It was said that a drop of rain at the edge of Lake Okeechobee would take over a year to make the slow journey south to the salt water.[3]

Fred Sr. was tough, had no money, and felt more at home living with the Seminoles than on Miami Beach. "In those days, the Everglades made the Wild West look like New York City!" Bill exclaimed while we spent an afternoon in his taxidermy studio in the mountains outside Franklin. "In south Florida, you were either a criminal or wanted to be one."

Bill's desk is littered with papers and photos of exotic places and forgotten times. A box of 416 Rigby cartridges is used as a paperweight, a subtle reminder of the caliber of dangerous game Bill pursued in Africa. Behind Bill's desk hang his grandfather's handmade knives and pistol. The knives were made from old files or saw blades. The handles are manatee rib bone. Next to them hangs a photo of his grandfather. There is nothing soft about the man in the photo. Hands like clubs hang from farm-strong arms. Several things in the photo stand out aside from the fact that Bill's grandfather was a physically imposing man. His darkened iron face is a hardened reflection of someone living beyond the edge of civilized society. Bill looked at the old photo, smiled, and said his grandfather's old buddies used to say, "Your grandpa, he was something else." And he was. "He used to swear there wasn't a man between Homestead and Key West who could whip his ass and would prove it every weekend, come home with bloodied knuckles and missing a tooth or two."

In the photo, Fred Sr. is standing outside the Homestead jail. His uncle was sheriff of Homestead and deputized his nephew, a job he did not keep long. Miami Beach in the '20s was a haven for rum-running and organized criminal activity during Prohibition. One night after receiving a tip about a shipment of liquor coming into Miami on a schooner, Fred Sr., holding the same .38-caliber pistol hanging behind Bill, found himself staring at several

Thompson submachine guns pointed right at him. "You with us or against us?" the mobsters asked Fred. His grandfather looked at the machine gun barrels and said calmly, "Where do you want it stacked?"

Fred Sr. was not formally educated, but he knew how to survive and was at home in the wild. Bill continued, "My grandfather lived with the Seminoles. He figured no one could find him out there if he didn't want them to." He also had an incredible agricultural prowess and even worked at the University of Miami as an instructor on how to graft plants. Due to his lack of formal education, he could not be a full-time professor, but he had a natural talent and skill. Bill added with pride, "There is even an avocado named after my grandfather, the Fuchs avocado."

Bill's older brother Bob followed his grandfather's passion of plants and today is arguably the most respected orchid grower in the world. A Bob Fuchs' orchid is a treasure desired by royalty and movie stars. Bill and Bob were competitive as kids. They grew violets under the benches in their family nursery. "Back then, we got fifty cents a violet, which was huge," Bill recalled. Bill, driven by sibling rivalry, blew up one of Bob's best violets one day with a firecracker, even though he knew he would get in trouble with his father.

Everglades National Park was established in 1947. Before that date, Bill's grandfather hunted everything from Flamingo to Homestead. To make a living, he hunted turkey and deer in the Everglades and would sell the meat to hotels and restaurants along Miami Beach. A good hunt might yield thirty or forty dollars. Once game laws were enacted in the national park, his hunting became poaching.

Homer Rhode was a game warden in those days. Like Fred Sr., Homer felt more at home immersed in the wildlife of the Everglades than around people. A giant man, at six feet five inches tall, Homer usually patrolled the swamps and wetlands by himself, working from a remote houseboat as a base. The two men formed an unusual relationship. Fred Sr., a poacher, and Homer, the game warden, both intricately connected to the Everglades, and both more knowledgeable of the Glades than anybody else.

Homer Rhode is a legendary figure in his own right. Homer's family moved from Pennsylvania to Coral Gables in the 1920s. His favorite early pastime was fly fishing the pristine limestone streams of eastern Pennsylvania, a passion he carried with him to south Florida.

Homer Rhode was one of the first fishermen to catch both a bonefish and permit on fly. The Homer Rhode Tarpon Streamer and Bucktail are credited for influencing many of the most famous saltwater flies in use today. Lee Wulff, the famous conservationist and fly fisherman, once wrote that the best fly he knew for bonefish was the Rhode shrimp fly. The Homer Rhode loop knot is still a staple of fly fishing instruction.

Ed Mitchell, an outdoor writer and photographer, has written numerous interesting articles about pioneering figures in saltwater fly fishing history, including Homer Rhode. Mr. Rhode was legendary for many things, including his uncanny ability to find snook. Mr. Mitchell notes in one of his articles that Homer Rhode would drive the Tamiami Trail at night, looking for dead leopard frogs on the road. He knew that where he found leopard frogs, there would be snook in the waters nearby. Fly fishing legend Lefty Kreh illustrates Homer Rhode's connection to the outdoors in an article interview with Ed Mitchell. Lefty quotes in the article:

> One night, Homer and I left his houseboat in a tin boat to do some fishing. Guided only by stars and the ink-black silhouette of the shoreline, Homer steered his boat through the labyrinth of the Ten Thousand Islands. Eventually,

we arrived at a spot loaded with snook. The
following morning, back at the houseboat, I
suggested a return trip. Homer paused and in
a quiet voice said we couldn't. He did not know
how to get there in the light of day.[4]

In the article Ed Mitchell wrote for *Fly Fishing in Salt Waters*
magazine, he offers intriguing perspective about the world and
wilderness in which Homer Rhode and Fred Fuchs, Sr. lived. He
describes the Everglades as "lawless and untamed as any place on
earth" with "clouds of mosquitoes thick enough to choke a horse."
He adds that the Everglades were "infested with criminals. At any
moment, you could be face-to-face with poachers, smugglers,
moonshiners, or even murderers."[5]

After his grandfather's passing, Bill Fuchs and Homer Rhode
became friends and eventually took several trips out west together.
During the long drives to Wyoming, Homer would tell Bill stories
about arresting his grandfather for trapping and poaching. Fred
Sr. trapped Everglades mink, for which he could get three dollars
a fur. He would also steal black or mottled duck eggs, which he
would hatch and raise to sell the meat. Each time Homer arrested
Fred Sr., he would tell him, "Don't do it again, Fred. I'm gonna bust
your ass." Sure enough, it wouldn't be long before Homer would
catch Fred Sr. again. During those long drives together, Homer
laughed as he told Bill great stories about chasing his grandfather
around the Everglades. "I had to put your grandfather in jail so
many times, I got tired of it."

Behind Fred Sr. in the photograph hanging near Bill's desk is the
Homestead jail. Lying in front of him in the photo is a fawn deer.
Just before the photo was taken, Fred Sr. was hunting deer and
shot a doe. While cleaning the doe, he felt movement and realized
the doe was pregnant with a fawn. He cut out the fawn, brought it
back to the Fuchs' home, and raised it on condensed milk. Bill has

pictures of his father, Fred Fuchs, Jr., as a child around the house with that same deer grown up.

Early settlements in the Everglades were regularly attacked by swarms of insects. The state offered land cheap to those who would drain and attempt to farm it; however, entire villages retreated when the swarms came. Some returned, only to be driven out again. Many would never come back.

"My grandfather was responsible for tending to the mule," Bill told me. "Every night, he had to cover the mule's face with a burlap croker sack to protect him from the mosquitos. One night, he forgot to cover the mule's face." That night, there was an unusual west wind, which brought droves of mosquitos. The next morning, he found the mule dead. "The mule's nostrils were blocked with thousands of dead mosquitos," Bill said. The mosquitos had swarmed the mule's bare face, filling his nasal cavity, and throat, by the thousands. The mule had suffocated to death.

"The mosquitos were a real problem in those days," Bill told me, "but so were the ants." Bill's family on his mother's side moved to Homestead as farmers in 1912. "They had to put the legs of their beds and kitchen table in old cans half-filled with kerosene, to keep the ants from covering them while they ate or slept." The ants would swarm during the rainy season, looking for dry or high ground and find the house. The ants would not cross the small moat of kerosene at the foot of each table or bed leg. "If you didn't have the kerosene, you would sleep in a bed of ants," Bill explained.

The Fuchs did not have electricity until 1941. One of the biggest challenges without electricity was preserving meat. Fred Sr. learned the Seminoles would keep cured meat by packing it in green pine needles. He applied what he learned and packed the family's cured hogs in pine needles. Sure enough, the meat did not spoil.

I asked Bill one time what the most important animal was to their family's early survival in the Everglades. He thought about it only briefly. "No question—the manatee." In the early days of settling the Glades, manatees were hunted for meat and oil, both critical to the survival of a family living in that remote wilderness.

Bill explained how they preserved manatee meat without electricity: "First, they had to get the manatee out of the canal. A manatee weighs twelve hundred or fifteen hundred pounds. If they couldn't get the manatee out of the canal, they would have to butcher it in sections so they could haul it back home. Once home, they would cut out the fat first and boil it in big black kettles. The bones would be saved for later to make tools. They would then take the red meat and slice it like you would beef into steak-sized pieces. The red meat would be fried until it was hard. Once hardened, and had no soft meat left to spoil, they would put it in a black pot and pour the liquid manatee oil in until that piece was covered."

They repeated this process of stacking and layering fried meat, then covering it in hot oil until the container was full and sealed. Once the container cooled, the oil solidified into thick grease, which preserved the meat. Bill added, "Manatee oil isn't like bear fat. Bear fat stays liquid after you have boiled it. It won't solidify again. Bear grease is liquid grease."

THE JUNGLE

In the '50s and early '60s, Bill Fuchs' family began exploring the jungles of Central and South America for new, exotic species of orchid they could bring back to their nursery near Homestead. As epiphytes, or "air plants," many orchid species sustain themselves in the rainforest canopy, far above the terrestrial ground. The orchids cling to the uppermost branches of the massive rainforest trees. Their roots grow out into the air, capturing moisture and nutrients from rainfall and debris that gather near their nesting place. This delicate location, often hundreds of feet above the cluttered forest floor, hides these living gems from intruders.

Bill's father, Fred Fuchs, Jr., learned the best way to access the orchids was to follow the loggers. As the logging companies felled trees deeper and deeper into the dense tropical forests, the Fuchs followed. The massive trees fell, bringing down with them new, exotic species of plants as well as insects and animals, which were living among the canopy. Once on the ground, the Fuchs collected the orchid specimens. Bill learned that among the orchids lived small deadly vipers, which he would try to catch. He carried them in thick currency sacks so the needle-like fangs could not puncture through to his skin.

When Bill and his two brothers were not helping their father with the orchids, they would head into the jungle with a fishing pole or shotgun and see what they could find. In addition to hunting snakes, Bill and his brothers hunted for tarantula. "We always carried a jar of peanuts to snack on in the jungle. When we finished the peanuts, we poked holes in the metal jar lid and used it to carry back tarantulas. We learned if we put too many smaller tarantulas in the jar, they would kill each other. So we were better off finding one big one."

Back in Florida, the Fuchs shared their home with gray foxes as well as monkeys and ocelots they'd brought back from Central America. Bill even raised a jaguar in his bedroom; it was a different time back then—South Florida was not developed like it is now, and areas around Homestead were still pretty remote. Curly, a woolly monkey Bill's father was particularly fond of, had run of the house. He slept with Bill's parents at night, pulling the sheets over himself like a child getting tucked in. Curly sat at the dinner table every evening, getting the seat of honor next to Bill's father. His favorite food was grapes. There was no quicker way for Bill or his brothers to get in trouble than to try and sneak one of Curly's grapes.

Less pampered than Curly were the resident Fuchs howler monkeys. They lived outside in cages around the yard. Bill recalled another time he was in serious trouble with his father. "I raised gray foxes in my bedroom," Bill said. "I trained them on leashes so they could be walked properly. The foxes would be lined up, each on a leash, and I walked them around the yard. Eventually, they became so used to the leashes they could be walked like any dog. One day, my dad had had enough of the foxes and told me it was time to get rid of them. I gathered them all together and put them in a basket on the front of my bike and rode out into the Everglades. I rode and rode, eventually finding an area I thought they could survive." The foxes were released, and Bill began the long ride home.

As he pulled back into his yard, his father was waiting for him. His father was obviously mad about something, and Bill desperately tried to think about what his father might have found that upset him. Mr. Fuchs brought out one of his prized howler monkeys, with a torn hand.

"Those damn foxes beat me back to the house," Bill laughed as he told me. "I took them so far out. It took me forever to ride all the way home, and they still beat me back to the house!" Evidently, the foxes ran back into the yard, arriving well ahead of Bill and his empty basket, and ran over to the howler monkey cage. The howler, who was not accustomed to seeing the foxes off their leashes, reached through the cage and tried to grab one of the loose canines. The fox, surprised at being suddenly grabbed, turned and bit the monkey's hand. Bill's father heard the commotion and, upon finding his injured pet, waited angrily for young Bill to return.

At first, the Fuchs focused their orchid exploration in Guyana, a small country east of Venezuela in South America. From Guyana, the Fuchs moved on to Bolivia, then Central America, including Nicaragua, which Bill described as "a bastion of good orchids." However, the most remote and wild place they ventured were the jungles of Ecuador. These were some of the most remote, unexplored jungles in the western hemisphere at that time. The grueling process of even getting to these remote, inhospitable areas was daunting. The Fuchs drove logging roads as far as they could, transferred to dugout canoe, then continued on foot. Pursuing orchids, or other treasure, meant pushing deeper and deeper into the jungles to the east, toward the very headwaters of the Amazon. That is where Bill first met the Jivaro.

The Jivaro are the indigenous people of the remote jungles of eastern Ecuador, where the eastern slope of the Andes meets the headwaters of the Amazon before it forms the mighty drainage downriver in Brazil. Bill's stories about those jungle rivers and the Jivaro were so foreign to anything I could imagine, it triggered my own research on the subjects. The Jivaro are secretive, with a long history of bravely defending their forest homes. They are known for their prowess with a blowgun, taking down birds and monkeys with poison-tipped darts. However, they may be best known for their practice of taking someone's full-size head and shrinking it down a size or two.

There were legends of gold being found in the mountains at the source of the deepest rivers of the Ecuadorian jungle. The Payamino was one of those rivers. I have read its eastern flow continues through Ecuador toward the Peruvian boarder, eventually joining the headwaters of the Amazon. Those adventurous enough would follow the Payamino upriver, panning for the precious golden residue in the silt. The Fuchs family followed this remote river, taking shelter at night with the indigenous people of the jungle.

The Jivaro are social, and visitors would be welcomed with a home-brewed beer called Nihamanchi, made from fermented manioc, or cassava roots. The manioc tubers are boiled and mashed. The Jivaro women then chew the soft mash, mixing it with their saliva, before spitting the liquid back into the pot. The saliva mix is then left to ferment. The resulting liquid tastes like an alcoholic buttermilk, and the local people may consume four or five quarts of the nutritious drink per day.[6]

The Fuchs were offered generous portions of Nihamanchi, followed by a meal of boiled monkey, which was cooked in a pot on a pile of sand in the middle of the hut. The hosting family would then lay a bed of banana leaves on the dirt, or bamboo floor, for their visitors to sleep on. It was considered insulting to not accept the food and drink offered by their native hosts, and Fred Fuchs led his family by example in joining in the meal.

As Bill sat on the shelter floor, watching his fascinating hosts, one of the men walked in carrying a sack. Three small, oddly shaped objects were laid at Bill's feet. At first, he thought they must be monkey skulls, used for ceremony. As he held them, studying them further, he realized they were not monkey skulls. They were human.

The shrunken heads were old, dried, and contorted into hideous expressions. The eyes were closed, long ago sewn shut after the skin was removed from the decapitated skull. The skull itself would have been discarded as a spiritual offering. The mouth would have been held together with palm pins, giving the face a jack-o-lantern expression. The resulting facial skin was boiled in tannin water to remove any fat and begin the shrinking process. Stones or wooden spheres would be used to mold the desired shape as the skin was dried with hot sand and rocks.[7,8]

The heads were laid at Bill's feet as an offering for trade. Bill was amazed at what he held but had nothing to trade, and the heads remained with their host. A missed opportunity, for a once-in-a-lifetime trade, that Bill regrets to this day.

Bill learned to hunt with the Jivaro, following their hunters deep into the forest with the sixteen-gauge he had carried with him from home. Their Jivaro hosts had never seen a real gun and were interested in what Bill carried. The only rifles occasionally brought up the river were homemade weapons mustered together from wire conduit. Of course, their skill with blowguns was undisputed. Bill witnessed firsthand their ability to shoot the poisoned blow darts over one hundred feet into the far reaches of the canopy, bringing down a wide variety of small game.

Their blowguns were finely tuned weapons, made from the wood of the chonta palm, split open and hollowed out with sand and water. The mouthpiece was bone, and the darts were made in mass by sharpening rigid palm leaves. The deadly part was the poison, applied to the tips of the darts. Unlike toxins rubbed from the skin of poison dart frogs in other parts of the Amazon, this poison was extracted from various plants. It was very effective. The toxin would enter the victim's bloodstream, paralyzing the diaphragm leading to death by asphyxiation.[9] One dart would result in one dead bird or monkey. Evidently non-toxic in the digestive system, the game was then gathered and returned to the family for cooking.

Bill followed the hunters deep into the forest. They would stop and listen, looking for telltale signs in the towering, dense leaf canopy. Once located, the animals were killed with expert precision. As a courtesy, Bill's "guides" finally let him use his unusual tool to take a shot at a group of birds. After the shot, the Jivaro saw something they had never seen before: three birds dropped at the shot instead of one. Bill, who was just in his late teens or early twenties at the time, had made his mark and earned some respect with this most unusual group of hunters. Bill returned to the village late in the day as a celebrated member of the hunting party.

The natives soon asked Bill to shoot macaws for them. They ate the birds and used the feathers as decoration. Most valued from the macaws, however, were their large, curved beaks, which the natives used to make eating utensils like spoons. Nothing went to waste.

"Did you know a bird-eating spider is so big, you can feel it crawling over your sleeping bag?" Bill asked me during one of our discussions in his taxidermy studio. I thought about his horrifying question and even though my response could have been a simple "no," I was a little afraid to answer. Bill's question did, however, spark my own memories of living in deep rainforests and jungle, where I faced the mental challenge of acclimatizing to the insects of that environment.

In my twenties, I became more involved in the sporting world, especially fly fishing. At that time, I lived in a small rundown apartment in Buckhead, Georgia, near Atlanta which, in those days, was an eclectic cluster of small streets lined with free flowing open door bars, reggae music, and a few shops. Across the street from my old apartment was the original location of The Fish Hawk, a venerable fly shop run by Gary and Bob Merriman and recognized by fly fisherman from all over the world as a go-to source of gear and advice. Every Friday and Saturday night, the streets around my apartment would be packed with a barrage of partiers, and every Saturday and Sunday morning, the streets would be littered with beer bottles and a few discarded remnants of the night before who fell into a dark corner instead of a cab. The beer bottles happened to be the same size and shape as a two-pound bonefish, even offering an implied "head" and swimming direction via the bottle neck. I was typically the first one awake in Buckhead those Saturday and Sunday mornings and walked the still sleeping streets, and parking lot of The Fish Hawk, casting my fly rod at beer bottles, pretending they were bonefish, practicing for the flats.

As I gained experience with a fly rod and expanded my connections with people and guides in that industry, I started getting invitations to join fly fishing excursions to various locations around the world, including deep into the Amazon and Yucatan jungles in pursuit of various fresh- and saltwater species of fish. I had loads of student debt and limited funds, but I saved money by living cheap and driving my old beater truck, which allowed me to tag along on those exciting trips. I never saw a live bird-eating spider in the Amazon, but I did see a dead one, and it was the size of my hand. Years later, and married with kids, as my wife and I expanded our efforts to escape the suburbs, we began a six-year stint of taking our kids to a remote eco-lodge in the undeveloped outer reaches of the Osa Peninsula of Costa Rica so they could experience the rainforest like I did in northeastern Australia back in grad school. The Osa, as well as Queensland, Australia, are the places I immersed myself among the jungle and its insects.

True virgin, meaning unlogged, rainforests and jungles are an alien place. Trees, and insects, grow to gargantuan scale. Leaves larger than a man block nearly all light from hitting the thick carpet of leaf litter on the jungle floor. Amazingly, in this world of giant plants, it's the tiny ants that keep the organic mass from suffocating itself. Leaf litter falling from the trees would eventually rise like a tide, swallowing the jungle and killing it, if it were not for the innumerable billions of ants, constantly breaking down the leaf matter, ebbing the tide.

One of the more intriguing species of ants from the jungles of Central America is the army ant. Unlike other ants, they do not build a permanent nest. Instead, the entire colony proceeds as one unit, forming living bivouacs as they move through the jungle. Army ant raids consume every living thing in their path. If the ants don't devour the prey on site, they carry the dismembered body with them to be eaten by the colony on the move or at the next bivouac.

There are stories about remote villages in Central America that welcome the raiding army ants to rid their homes of unwanted pests. When the ants arrive, the villagers, and hopefully their pets, clear out of their houses. The ants come right through, driving or carrying every roach, scorpion, or snake from the house. Nothing is left behind. The ants move on, and the villager has a clean house.

I have seen just one colony of army ants on the move, probably ten years ago, while I was out jogging on a trail in the Osa, and I will not forget it. It was a flowing river of ants, about two feet in width, crossing a dirt jungle path in front of me. I stood in amazement, only a foot from the edge of the torrent, for fifteen minutes. The surge of movement never slowed. More incredible than the sight was the sound, a never ending clatter of a million tiny bodies, surging as one organism across the jungle floor, eating everything in their path.

The Osa Peninsula of Costa Rica is close to the Panamanian border. The outer reaches, where we stayed, have no paved roads or electricity. I recall reading an article where *National Geographic* referred to the Osa as the "most biologically intense place on Earth."[10] Our cabin was open-air to the surrounding jungle, which teemed with life. We drank rainwater collected in a cistern. Our family's first night in the jungle was terrible. Everyone, including myself, was afraid to sit down or touch anything with fear of something crawling out. The second night was better than the first and by the third or fourth night, we all began to relax and embrace the jungle and its critters.

One year, a giant golden orb spider spun a web next to the front door of the cabin. Golden orb webs are big. They have to be to support the spider itself, which can be over five inches in length, let alone its prey, which could be insects, reptiles, or even small birds. We left the spider alone. Eventually, it became part of the charm of the small house, and the kids started feeding it lizards. Inside the cabin, geckos were constantly crawling all over the walls and ceiling. Geckos make a surprisingly loud shrill call, which at first scared everyone to death. Again, after a few days of settling in, and realizing the geckos were eating far worse things than geckos, the shrill sound became a comfort, especially at night. Over the years at that remote eco-lodge, we found everything from scorpions to tarantulas to numerous venomous snakes near the cabin and, for the most part, fear eventually turned to interest.

Back in grad school, our campus was a research center deep in the rainforest of northern Queensland, Australia. Queensland has some of the oldest tropical rainforest on earth. While true rainforest differs from jungle due to the high canopy of trees, they are similar. The rainforest hits you with an intensity of sounds and smells you can't anticipate. The very edge of the jungle forest is an imposing dark wall impervious to light. Our campus had two or three single-story buildings providing a classroom, open area, and kitchen. We had two professors and an intern, who acted as guides, and a few additional staff members. The fifteen or so students were housed in small cabins farther back in the forest.

We drank rainwater gathered from the roof via a maze of gutters and tubes, eventually collecting in large barrels, from which we would scoop out pitchers of water. As the water sat in the barrels, it attracted mosquitos, which laid their eggs in it. On average, a pitcher of our drinking water probably contained several hundred living, swimming mosquito larvae. At first, this repulsed every student in the school, including myself. The efficiency of thirst however wins every time, and we learned to stop looking in our cups. One of my classmates came up with the brilliant idea to mix powdered orange Tang in the pitchers, which camouflaged most of the larvae. Like everything, we eventually just got used to it and drank the water, larvae and all, right from the barrels.

The rainforest surrounded our campus, which meant our little cabins were regularly home to oversized crawling things. The wooden structures were basic: a few bunks, one or two cots, a hanging light overhead, and screened windows, which let in all the sounds of the jungle. I checked my sleeping bag every night before going to bed and slept with a Maglite flashlight next to my cot. After carefully checking my sleeping bag the first night for critters, I crawled in. Our cabin light was turned out, and the forest night was pitch black. The southern-cross constellation was framed overhead in a screened window. I was not yet used to the sounds of the forest at night, especially the flapping of leather wings from giant fruit-eating bats, or appropriately named flying foxes. A few of the locals told us about college kids farther south who kept flying foxes as pets. The giant bats would crawl up into their bed at night and sleep with their owners like dogs. During the day, the kids carried their bats around campus hanging from their arms like leather purses.

After settling into my sleeping bag, I reached for my flashlight to have one last look in the dark. I switched on the small light and swept the tight beam along the wall above my cot. Right next to my head was the face of the largest huntsman spider I have ever seen. Australia's horrifying funnel web spiders are thankfully uncommon in the northern rainforest; however, we did have plenty of big huntsman spiders. The huntsman is not venomous, but it's one of the world's largest predator spiders, with fangs you would rather not meet. The one staring at me was bigger than the palm of my hand, and surprisingly thick. In the light, the spider's face was big enough—and close enough—that I could clearly see each of the individual eight eyes reflecting back at me.

It—I don't know if it was a he or she, nor did I care—had come out to hunt at night and was hanging on the side of the wall about a foot above my head. I was too scared to move, and I really didn't want to startle the spider. Instead, I lay there and just looked up at it for about ten minutes. It never moved. Eventually, I had to make the daunting decision to turn out the flashlight and try to get some sleep. I turned out the light and grimaced, imagining that giant spider falling on my face in the darkness. I kept telling myself the spider was looking for other things to eat, not me. After an eternity, I finally feel asleep. I woke early the next morning and looked up. The spider was gone. He came back every night, right above my cot, for weeks. Eventually, I stopped turning on my flashlight to look at him. In a crazy sort of way, I looked forward to seeing him each night. I figured nothing else would bother me in the dark with that huge spider right above my head.

Each morning during our first week in the jungle, I wrapped my safari pants in duct tape over my boots like an NFL trainer to protect myself from the leeches, spiders, and other creepy-crawly things in the rainforest. Fear eventually subsided and, by the second week in the bush, I was wearing shorts and going barefoot. For the record, my duct tape did not keep out the leeches.

The leeches were relentless in their pursuit of bare human skin. My first day in the field, we took water samples from a small jungle creek. I was wearing my full-length field pants, tightly wrapped with duct tape. The following morning, I was sitting in class. The classroom was a bare room with a concrete floor and large screened windows. There were four or five rows of folding tables with basic student chairs. I wore the same pants from the day before, which had dried in the sun. As I sat in class, I felt something on my leg. I looked down. In the middle of my upper thigh, under my pants, was an unnervingly large raised lump. I thought for a moment about what my next move should be. Jumping out of the chair, screaming, and dropping my pants in class had merit and seemed like the logical thing to do. However, after thinking it further through, I realized that whatever it was on my leg, I really did not want to startle it. Instead, I slowly pulled a penknife from my pocket and began to cut my pants open right above the lump.

Our professor, unaware of my little drama, continued his lecture on symbiotic relationships among rainforest species. I cut a long strip down my pants and pulled back the material. On my upper thigh was a huge leech engorged with my blood. This prompted another moment of thought about what to do next. I carefully pulled the swollen leech from my skin, dropped it on the floor under my table, and crushed it with my foot. Kind of like stepping on a small water balloon. I don't recall if anyone sitting around me even noticed the event as it occurred, but I had a heck of a bloody mess to clean up after class.

Let's go back to Bill Fuchs's question: "Did you know a bird-eating spider is so big, you can feel it crawling over your sleeping bag?" *Theraphosa blondi*, or the bird-eating spider, is the largest spider in the world by mass, second only in leg span to the cave-dwelling giant huntsman spider of southeast Asia, which can attain sizes of a full foot across.[11,12] Also known as goliath bird eaters, *blondi*'s leg span reaches eleven inches, but it is their body's mass that dwarfs all other arachnids. At six ounces, they weigh almost half a pound.

When the Fuchs were following the Rio Payamino deep into northeastern Ecuador, they made camp on a split bamboo platform long ago vacated by a Jivaro family. The platform was raised to keep the dwelling above high water. The floor was sturdy but "spongy," as Bill recalled. More importantly, the raised platform provided a barrier to the crawling armies of insects on the jungle floor. The platform had a palm-thatched bamboo roof, which was well-built and provided shelter from rain. However, the hollow bamboo attracted giant roaches, which in turn attracted giant tarantulas that hunted the roaches at night.

Sometimes you are better off not knowing what lurks in the darkness. Bill knew better than to step off the platform at night. The first evening, he wished he had never even turned on his flashlight. Hundreds of eyes reflected back. Spider eyes reflect light. The jungle around the Fuchs's platform was crawling with tarantulas. They were in the trees and on the ground. Some were too immense to imagine. The only thing worse than turning the light on was turning it back off. The impenetrable rainforest canopy blocks all light from the moon. It was in this black of blackness that Bill crawled back into his sleeping bag and closed his eyes. "At night," Bill recalled, "there were things on that platform you did not want to even think about." The giant tarantulas would explore the camp for prey—roaches, other insects, frogs, or even small mammals. They were big enough to make a slight sound as they crawled across the forest floor, but would be silent on the platform. "As hot as it was, you would pull that sleeping bag and zip it all the way up and hope you suffocated," Bill said. "You could feel their weight, their feet on you. You just wanted to huddle in that bag until morning."

AFRICA

Bill Fuchs spent his childhood exploring the jungles of Central and South America, but he and his wife Linda have spent their adult years hunting and outfitting in Africa.

Bill married Linda in 1973, relocating their taxidermy studio from a chicken coop in Mobile, Alabama, to the mountains of western North Carolina in 1976. Like others in this book, she is very unassuming. Linda's smile is warm and proud as she welcomes visitors to their studio, and her interest is sincere as she listens to their recent hunting successes. If you look closer at the studio, you see many of the largest dangerous game animals were taken by Linda. Her record book cape buffalo and brown bear glare down at visitors. The Fuchs's studio has multiple layers. It's easy to notice the big game hanging from the walls. However, if you look closer, you see smaller pieces, which tell even more incredible tales of a different time and place.

The Fuchs hunted Africa extensively, primarily in Tanzania. Over the years, their interest in Africa expanded into an outfitting and guide business, including photographic safaris in Zimbabwe. Bill's perspective on the wonders and horrors of Africa is from firsthand accounts. He lost two friends to gruesome cape buffalo mauling. "Buffalo will kill you; lion will eat you," Bill said. "The scariest sounds are coming in on feeding lion at night," he noted, describing the guttural sounds of low growling, tearing meat, and breaking bones. Bill added, "But the leopard sounds are the most intense."

West Nicholson, in Southwest Zimbabwe, is located on the banks of the Mzingwane River, a tributary of the famous Limpopo River. The region is well known for mopani woodland, granite hills (or "koppies"), and big leopard. One night, Linda and her guide, referred to as a "professional hunter," or "PH" in Africa, were in a blind on a big cat. Bill and the trackers made camp over a mile behind them as to not disturb the blind. Bill made a small campfire of mopani wood. "Mopani is the best wood for camp fires while hunting in the bush," Bill noted. "It burns clean and does not snap." Bill and the two trackers were sitting around the small fire, looking up at the dark African sky. They would stay there all night, or until they received a call on the radio from Linda's PH, giving them an update from the leopard blind. Bill could not sleep anyway. He was excited for Linda's opportunity as they could tell based on tracks this was a big leopard.

Suddenly, in the darkness, the baboons started barking, jolting Bill and the trackers to their senses. They were not expecting this. They had purposefully made camp far from the blind to eliminate any chance of intercepting the male leopard. It was just bad luck the big cat happened to come in from their direction.

Bill looked at me and smirked. "The baboons were going crazy. Everybody knows the big man is on the move … shit is about to happen." Bill and the two trackers did not move. Leopards do not tend to make noise as they approach a kill. However, as I have been told by a few friends, if a big leopard knows you are there, they make a sound that is one of the most intense in Africa. Matobo Hills PH and author Wayne Grant notes in his book *Into the Thorns*, "It is a primal, hair raising sensation if you are ever close to a calling leopard." Mr. Grant describes the sound as a "sawing, hollow, pig-like grunting."[13] Bill described it as follows: "It sounded like someone was trying to start a chainsaw, the sound you make pulling the starter rope." Bill and the two trackers did not move as that sound passed right by them, just feet from the edge of the campfire light. Bill knew it was the big male. Linda and her PH never saw the big cat that night. The next morning, the tracks, also known as "spoor," told the story. The male did come to the bait, but it never showed itself. It watched a smaller female feed instead. Smart, old cat.

Bill once told me a story about the harsh reality of sleeping out in the African bush. Paul Jelonek was a PH from Zimbabwe. He recently passed away from cancer but was a good friend of the Fuchs for many years, even moving to the Franklin area of North Carolina later in life. Paul served in the Rhodesian War. He and a friend had been on patrol for days. One night, they were ordered on point to identify locations being used for river crossings. After patrol, they established a rough bivouac near the river and fell asleep exhausted. Paul woke early the next morning. His friend, who was sleeping right next to him, was gone. "He had been dragged from his sleeping pad by a hyena," Bill said. "His skull had been crushed. That's how powerful and sinister the hyena is." Bill relayed, "The hyena had smelled him, sniffed him, grabbed him by the head, and crushed him, precluding him from making any sound." Paul, sleeping just feet away, never woke until the following morning when he found his dead friend in the brush with a crushed skull, surrounded by hyena tracks.

I hunted Africa with my close friend, and gifted outdoor writer, Jimmy Ewing. The hyenas were always there, circling, cleaning up. You constantly feel their presence in Africa. Their whooping calls haunt you at night. In the early mornings, as you drive the dirt roads looking for fresh spoor, chasing the escaped asylum of guinea fowl and kicking away tire damaging rocks rolled onto the road the night before by troops of baboons looking for scorpions, the hyena tracks are always there.

Nothing goes to waste in the African bush. The lions eat first, then the hyenas, then the vultures and eagles, then the jackals and the ants and so on. We found a dead elephant one morning in Zimbabwe. It was a younger bull, probably ten or twelve years old. The ivory was intact. It had died of natural causes, or a snake bite, not poachers. The body was bloated, but there, save the organs, which had been fed upon by three lions we spooked as we approached. The next morning it was a pile of stiff, dried skin. In just one winter day (July), Africa consumed the entire elephant. We hung hyena baits, and got some incredible trail cam photos of the hyenas coming in at night. One afternoon, Jimmy and his PH hung a bait of zebra ribs along a small spring. An abandoned camp sat high on a hill, three hundred yards from the bait, offering the perfect vantage. The old camp was unnervingly empty, except for three bushmen, who the land concession owner asked to remain to kill mambas and keep baboons from taking over the camp. Surprisingly, the bait sat untouched for a few days. It was the African winter, and baits lasted longer than during the hot summers, when flies turn hung meat into soup within a day or two. Eventually the bait was taken down, but not before the meat was removed and eaten by the bushmen living at the camp.

A massive crocodile swept across one wall of the Fuchs's studio in Franklin. The croc was one of two man-eaters identified by local authorities as having killed and eaten seven Maasai villagers along the banks of the Kilombero River in Tanzania. The river forms the Kilombero Valley, one of the greatest wetlands of East Africa, eventually flowing through the famous Selous game reserve. It is known for fertile tributaries filled with fish, and enormous Nile crocodiles.[14]

Each year the Nile crocodile is responsible for hundreds of attacks and human deaths in rural Africa. In reality, many attacks are never reported, so actual numbers are probably higher than records show. The hippo is also considered one of Africa's most

118 R<small>IDR</small> K<small>NOWLTON</small>

dangerous and deadly animals however, there is question about whether some of the deaths attributed to hippos are, in fact, caused by crocodiles. According to professional hunters I have spoken with, when an attack occurs, the villagers search for the body by dragging the river bottom with weighted hook thorn bushes behind boats. The hook shaped thorns will catch the body. When a death is reported, the government authorities arrive at the village to "kill" the maneater. If the village reports the attack was from a hippo the authorities shoot the first big hippo they find. They then give the meat to the village. A hippo provides significantly more meat to a village than a crocodile. This incents the reporting of an attack by hippo instead of crocodile, some believing the number of crocodile attacks may in fact be up to fifty percent higher than reported.

I learned first hand how sudden and powerful the attack from a submerged crocodile can be. I was hunting a small riverbed in the Matetsi area of Northwestern Zimbabwe with PH, Chap Esterhuizen. Chap is from Bulawayo, not far from the Matobo Hills and West Nicholson, the area noted earlier for big leopard. Chap is a real bushman. As a leopard hunter, his awareness of the natural surroundings is absolute, and needs to be to outsmart one of the most wary and crafty animals on earth.

Chap and I had some downtime on a recent cape buffalo hunt and decided to spend a few days scouting for possible blind locations for an upcoming leopard hunt Chap had scheduled. Like with most of the guides in this book, the "hunting" is occurring well before the client arrives, when the professional hunter locates and prepares the perfect combination of bait, obstacle and blind. I don't personally have an interest in hunting leopard, but I fully appreciate the knowledge, science and strategy required to be a successful leopard hunter, and jumped at the opportunity to follow Chap and his team of trackers and scouts as they assessed various river bottoms for potential locations to set up blinds. An added benefit was the same river bottoms were also prime habitat for bushbuck, a challenging antelope we were also hunting. As I followed Chap and his team along a small river, which eventually fed the Matetsi River, the scout whistled for us to stop. He spotted a decent sized crocodile about two hundred yards ahead sunning itself on matted grass up on the riverbank. We were in thick cover, but the crocodile's ability to see, hear and smell at distance is legendary, so we all took care to not move or make a sound. Chap has an uncanny skill of calling animals, almost speaking with them. Turkey hunters back home do the same, but Chap does it without a call. He just uses his mouth. I have watched him do this with birds, hyenas, various antelope ... and crocodile. Chap made a few crocodile hatchling vocalizations directed downriver, toward the sunning croc. These calls are typically made by baby crocs as they are hatching. Since the hatchling's call can also attract predators, adult crocodiles in the immediate area may instinctively respond to the sound, trying to provide protection to the hatching babies.

On his second call, the crocodile threw itself into the river and began swimming toward us. The croc was swimming so hard and fast toward Chap's calls, its head was elevated above the water and it pushed a deep wake in the river. Our small group remained still as the croc quickly cut the distance from two hundred yards to one hundred, then fifty, then twenty-five. The muddy riverbank below us was steep, and a good four feet in height, so I assumed there was no danger of the croc scaling the bank to where we stood. As the ten-foot croc cut the distance further, Chap subtly adjusted his calling. The croc turned directly toward us. None of us moved. I was amazed he had called this crocodile in from over two hundred yards, better than any gobbler I have seen. The crocodile pushed itself right to the edge of the river, its wake making a notable sound in the water, stopping directly below us and temporarily out of sight. There was suddenly silence. Nothing happened for two or three seconds. Then the three hundred pound crocodile exploded out of the water, over the bank and at us. We were no more than three feet away. Chap was closest to the river. I was directly behind him at his shoulder. I vividly recall seeing the crocodile turn its head to the side as it opened its jaws and went for our legs. I stepped back five or six feet. Chap stood his ground, holding the barrel of his .500 Nitro Express double rifle out in front him, the tip of the barrel no more than six inches from the jaws of the charging croc. Chap yelled twice at the croc, a strategy used by professional hunters to try and turn charging dangerous game rather than having to resort to shooting or injuring the animal. Incredibly, Chap did not shoot the croc. By holding his ground, and yelling, Chap turned the crocodile at the last second. The big animal spun its body around, the tail whipped by us, and it flung itself off the riverbank into the water and disappeared. It was over in a few seconds. Chap, myself, the native trackers, scouts and game official all looked at each other with the universally understood "holy shit" expression, and exhaled simultaneously. The native scout, a tall thin quiet man who tended to walk slowly through the bush with both hands clasped behind his back like a professor evaluating projects at a science fair, then spoke in his native tongue. As we walked away in silence, I asked Chap what he had said. Chap smiled, "He said … 'now THAT was the first interesting thing I have seen all year.'" Later, as we made it back to the two track road and Rover, Chap commented "I sure am glad I did not have to shoot that croc. It was probably a female, just coming to protect babies. It was just doing its job."

"A croc is not like an alligator," Bill Fuchs told me. "An alligator will spot you across a canal, but a croc will spot you [from] well down a river." A large crocodile can see, smell, and sense unwanted eyes at an almost mystical distance. A crocodile can feel the vibrations of someone walking the bank of the river. A stalk on an apparently lazy, dozing croc can be a long, painfully deliberate process, typically resulting in submersion by the animal.

I have spooked both alligators in Florida, and crocodiles in Africa but, as Bill noted, "Comparing an alligator to a crocodile is like comparing a cumquat to a Mercedes. They have nothing to do with each other ... an alligator you can walk up and kick that son of a bitch in the head or grab its tail. A crocodile, if you move at a hundred yards he has seen you, and he is gone." Bill acknowledges he does not understand this behavioral difference in the two animals, as the Nile crocodile has not been persecuted like the American alligator. A big Nile croc is the undisputed king of its world. "I don't know why the croc is so wide awake," Bill noted, "but he is."

The Nile crocodile's larger cousin, the saltwater crocodile, was regularly on my mind in Australia. I once heard the giant saltwater crocodile was referred to as the "King of its world on both land and water," referring to its ability and willingness to attack and eat large sharks along the Australian coast. My grad school's research trips included locations along the coast of Queensland as well as interior estuaries and lakes. I recall a story in the news while I was there about the police department having to call off a search-and-rescue effort along the coast due to the dangerous number of saltwater crocodiles. By the time they were able to access the location, it was too late.

"It's the dead ones that kill you" is a well-earned proverb of African dangerous game, and it has been relayed to countless hunters as they approach supposedly dead animals. Horror stories abound of mortally wounded lion, leopard, and, of course, cape buffalo coming back to life before being poked in the eye.

Rob Lurie, a friend and well known professional hunter in Zimbabwe was recently hunting the lowveld of the Bubye Valley in southeastern Zimbabwe. Rob and his client were tracking a wounded buffalo in the thick jesse, which charged them from ten yards. Both shot as the bull erupted from the bush, neither bullet stopping the charge. Rob shot again at five yards, dropping the big bull, which reared back like a horse before falling. The buffalo was down, or so they hoped. Rob instinctively reloaded his double rifle just as the "dead" buffalo came back to life for a final swing. The client's gun jammed, and Rob managed a well placed shot at three yards which finally anchored the bull.

Rob told me about another buffalo that had to be shot sixteen times. "That buffalo died of lead poisoning," Rob jested. According to Rob, buffalo have much higher releases of adrenaline than humans when injured, allowing a "dead" buffalo to charge.

Africa holds untold stories of the rage and mayhem of cape buffalo coming back to life, however, of all the big game, I can't imagine any that rival Crocodylia's unwillingness to give up the ghost and ability to come back from being stone-dead. Legendary professional hunter and author Peter Hathaway Capstick sums it up in his classic *Death in the Long Grass* when he writes, "'A croc ain't dead until the hide's salted, and even then don't count on it!'"[15]

Caiman are a cousin to the American alligator and native to Central and South America. While some species are able to reach lengths exceeding fifteen feet, they are incomparably less aggressive and dangerous than a Nile crocodile and don't even warrant discussion in the same chapter. That said, my minimal personal experience with these critters coming back to life is limited to these less dangerous and typically smaller reptiles.

Like the alligator, caiman meat is quite good and prized among local fisherman. I accompanied native caiman hunters at night while fishing the Rio Negro in the Amazon during those fishing trips in my twenties. One hunter paddles the low canoe; the other leans forward over the front holding a blunt weapon. They paddle along the dark riverbanks looking for reflecting eyes. Once they've spotted such eyes, they slowly paddle toward them, approaching in the dark. The hunter in front waits until the bow of the canoe is alongside the unexpecting caiman. They then stun it with a heavy blow. The stunned caiman, typically no more than five or six feet long, is then lifted into the canoe and finished off. Once dispatched, the reptile is tossed into the lowest central part of the canoe, where I sat. If I got covered in, let's say, seven or eight caiman during the evening hunt, by the time we got back to camp later that night, I would wager that none were dead. The hunters would pull out the very much alive and agitated caiman from the bottom of the canoe, along with me, also agitated, and re-dispatch the caiman for the second time.

Let's go back to the huge croc hanging in Bill Fuch's studio. Efforts to trap the crocodiles attacking the Maasai village had failed. The Maasai wanted a hunter to bring an end to the killings, and authorities issued two permits to hunt and kill the man-eaters. Bill's PH Paul Jelonek was given one of the permits and invited the Fuchs to begin scouting for the massive crocodiles.

Bill, Paul, and their local tracker Mozango scoured the Kilombero River. They saw plenty of crocodile, but at first, not the half-ton maneaters they were looking for. They continued to glass long stretches of riverbanks. Eventually, they spotted in the far distance an enormous crocodile on the opposite side of the river. They realized they must be looking at one of the man-eaters. After a long, slow, quarter-mile crawl, they peered over the bank and saw the massive croc lying across the river on a sandbar, right at the water's edge. Paul whispered to Bill, "Do you think you can get him, Bill?" Bill replied, "Yeah, I can get him."

The crocodile was about one hundred twenty-five yards across the water. Paul whispered, "Shoot him behind the smile."

What Bill's guide meant was the location of the quarter-sized target where you need to hit a croc in the brain or spine to kill it instantly. It is arguably the smallest target, and most challenging shot to take, in the hunting world.

Bill carefully took the shot. "It happened very quick," Bill recalled. "I heard the *pow*, *whap* of the shot. I could see the sand pop over the croc's head, and the croc went in the river." Linda and their daughter Corie were both back in camp, about a half-mile downriver. Bill had asked them to not leave the camp for safety measure, but when they heard the shot, they both went running down the path. The poor guy who was supposed to be watching them at camp didn't stand a chance. Bill laughed, "You don't tell my wife 'no.' When he asked Linda to stay back, she said, 'Bullshit, we're gone.'" Bill added, "It was quite a snaky place, and they encountered two snakes running down that path, but made it down to where I was."

Bill told Linda he did not know where the croc was and thought he may have missed it. Bill felt disgusted with himself, thinking he had missed the croc. They had traveled for hours to establish a new camp near where they thought they would have the best chance to spot the man-eaters, and Bill was concerned he had blown it. Suddenly, one of the trackers whispered, "There he is … there he is." The big croc had surfaced and was moving slowly along the edge of the river. Paul whispered, "Bill, try him again." Bill's second shot anchored the big croc, but it slowly sank into the river. "The river's flowing pretty big, and I was afraid I had lost the croc. I sat there and thought to myself, 'Well shit, now what do we do?'" The croc was on the opposite side of the river and had now disappeared. There were also about twenty hippo in the river, all irritated at the gunshots flying over their heads, laying partially submerged right between Bill and where the crocodile had gone under.

They decided to grab a fiberglass canoe from camp. Paul spotted a fisherman down on the same side of the river as the croc. They carried the canoe down to the river's edge. Paul yelled across to the fisherman in native tongue, who agreed to help find the crocodile. Bill, his rifle, Paul, and Mozango all piled into the small fiberglass canoe. "I didn't tie a string to the rifle; I figured if I went over, I would just hang on to it," he recalled. "We paddled right through those hippos. It would be placid water, and one of the big hippos would suddenly appear right next to the low canoe, making their warning bellows—*whaawhaawhaawhaa*—and then go back down." He continued, "You don't know what the next one's gonna do. The most intimidating thing was getting through those hippos ... we get to the other bank and the fisherman gets his mud pole and starts poking around in the river."

The fisherman suddenly stopped and began speaking excitedly to Paul. Paul looked at Bill and pointed to the fisherman. "He found him. He's right there." The problem was that they did not know if the croc was dead or alive and which way it was facing—in other words, where were the teeth? The river was muddy and even though the croc was only submerged three or four feet, it was completely hidden in the cloudy water. The savvy fisherman knew what to do. He grabbed his mud pole and began rubbing the pole along the length of the submerged croc. A crocodile has ridges along its back, which aim toward the tail. The fisherman was bush smart and knew this; he used his cane pole in the muddy water to feel which way the ridges along the crocodile's massive back were angled. The fisherman stood up and proclaimed to Paul, "The head is this way. The tail is this way."

Bill looked at me and said, "This is where the savvy bush people can exceed anybody on Wall Street for common sense! They don't know shit about the stock market, but by god they know something about nature and how to survive!"

At this point, they knew where the croc was and where its head and tail were. The problem was whether it was dead or alive. The riverbank was steep, offering only four or five feet of space to deal with an angry croc. Bill continued, "Suddenly, the fisherman goes completely under water ... there was a bit of a pause ... a bit of *what's gonna happen next*, and then he comes up holding the crocodile's tail. We all started hooting and hollering and dragged the crocodile up on the bank, hoping he was dead."

The maneater was dead. They emptied all the water out of the canoe, rolled the crocodile into the small boat, and paddled the croc, then themselves, back to the other bank. Thankfully, the hippos had moved on.

The local Maasai celebrated the death of one of the killer crocs. They hung the thousand pound croc from a tree back in camp for an unforgettable portrait with the Fuchs. In the photo, Bill, kneeling, holds the tail, which just dusts the ground in front of him. Linda and Corie stand nearby. The rear legs of the croc hang over their heads, showing how big it really was. They skinned the croc in camp. The Maasai, still excited about the demise of the first man-eater, feared the crocodile's liver, believing it would bring bad karma to the village. As such, they did not want the crocodile to be gutted. Just a few days after the Fuchs left camp, another hunter killed the second man-eater in the Kilombero. It was also massive. This time, the crocodile was gutted on the riverbank, prior to being brought to the village. The PH sent Bill the photos, which I have seen. They are gruesome and confirm the crocodiles were indeed maneaters. A partially digested human leg, arm, and hand, among other recognizable body parts, are clearly visible next to the crocodile carcass.

Bill thought about the crocodile for a moment. He mentioned he wished he could have gotten his crocodile rocks. "I wanted my crocodile rocks—that is the real prize of Africa. A crocodile, what they call a "flat dog," ingests rocks that suit him, much like an ostrich or chicken, which aid in the mastication of food," Bill explained. A crocodile tears off large chunks of its prey by rolling it in the "death roll." The chunks of prey are swallowed whole. The first step of digestion is the "chewing" of food, or mastication. Because the crocodile does not chew—instead, it tears—mastication occurs through food being ground up by the rocks in a crocodile's stomach. Not only do these rocks aid in the mastication of the croc's food, they also serve as a ballast format, helping the crocodile maintain balance in the water.

Bill explained it to me like this: "In a crocodile's lifetime of sixty to eighty years, he has ingested a hat full of special rocks. Once they stay in his gut all this time, through the mastication of food, they are polished to an unbelievable sheen, like a cabochon gemstone. They are soft and round and beautiful—you could even find a two-pound tanzanite." He added, "I don't give a shit if you have a Van Gogh in your house. If you have a woven Maasai basket made by one of the village ladies with crocodile rocks in it, now that's a conversation piece."

Bill was angry he did not get his crocodile rocks. He tells me early South African diamond explorers learned they could shoot ostrich and find diamonds in the grit in the bird's craw, similar to the crocodile stones. "An ostrich, over its fifty-plus-year lifespan, covers a lot of open terrain picking up and swallowing pretty rocks, like a chicken does." He added, "Those early prospectors could shoot an ostrich, eat the bird, and then pull diamonds from the grit in the craw without having to mine. They left a carnage of ostrich across Africa, not unlike shooting buffalo [in America] just for their tongues."

SNAKES

When you're sitting around a hunting or fishing camp, it's only a matter of time before the snake stories come out. "Rattlesnakes as big around as your arm" and "moccasins that drop out of trees into your bass boat" are classic tales and always a camp highlight. Whether a phobia or not, snakes live in the recesses of a sportsman's mind, and they have an indelible connection with many of us in the sporting world.

Individual reactions to snakes differ based on interest, fear, or even repulsion. But they all share some form of fascination. It's a fascination similar to that of sharks. Basically, things we don't really understand but believe can cause us harm. Even more so, it's a fascination of what we believe can cause us harm that we cannot see. The shark is typically not seen, yet it is there, even if just in our imagination. The same goes for snakes. We don't regularly see them, yet our imagination fills the outdoors with dangerous snakes.

I knew this book would have plenty of snake stories, but I got the idea of dedicating a chapter to the subject from reading Peter Hathaway Capstick, once again from his book *Death in the Long Grass*. In the '60s, Mr. Capstick left a career on Wall Street to become a professional hunter. His hunting career began in the jungles of Central and South America, culminating in Central Africa. His books are classics, and they tell harsh and thrilling tales from both his personal experiences deep in the bush as well as accounts of other legendary hunters of bygone eras. In particular, *Death in the Long Grass* recounts incredible tales of the various dangerous game of the African continent. Graphic and insightful accounts of the African Dangerous Seven—or lion, elephant, leopard, cape buffalo, hippo, crocodile, and rhino—are told in chapters one through seven accordingly. It was chapter eight, "Snakes," that caught my eye when I first read his book, and I turned to those pages first, where Mr. Capstick describes the month of October, the beginning of the African summer, as being notable for more than "heat rash and tempers." He states, "October is the first month of snakes."[16]

A quail hunter in southwest Georgia does not want to step on a rattlesnake or moccasin. Nor does a turkey hunter want to sit on a copperhead, and none of us want to meet a mamba on an African safari. Those situations are unlucky encounters, typically with the hunter unknowingly entering the personal space of the snake, who defends itself. Over the years, I have had many encounters with dangerous snakes but, with the exception of one aggressive moccasin in southern Alabama who stood his ground and then some, every one of those snakes just wanted to get away from me.

When I was younger, I was fascinated with snake stories. My dad went to the University of Miami. In those days, he and his buddies would drive out the Tamiami Trail and take buggies into the Everglades at night to hunt wild boar and raid alligator nests looking for baby alligators to sell back in Miami. One night, they came across an enormous diamondback rattlesnake that stretched across a canal access road. I am quite certain neither my father nor his pals were sober enough that night to tangle with a big diamondback, and luckily they parted ways, but that story stuck with me as a kid. I wanted desperately to have my own rattlesnake story. Ironically, the more I looked for rattlesnakes in the bush, trying to force the encounter, the longer it took to finally see one. It was probably ten years later, only after I had stopped looking for them, when I finally saw my first venomous snake, a canebrake rattlesnake on a south Georgian road.

My first encounter with a big diamondback was a few years later, during early bow season in southeast Georgia. I was using a climbing stand and had shimmied up a tall, thin pine tree that sat along a well-marked deer trail, set about thirty yards back in the trees from an open field. I climbed the tree, hoping to get a shot at an early-season doe I thought might come into the field to feed late in the afternoon. About an hour after settling into the swaying tree, I heard movement. Several minutes passed without seeing anything on the trail. Moments later, I heard it again. It did not sound like a deer. It wasn't the sound of a cautious step, and I considered it might be wild pigs. I had climbed pretty high that day, at least high for myself, maybe twenty feet above the ground. High enough to have a good look at the surrounding underbrush and a clear view of the trail. Still nothing. I heard the sound again, this time not more than thirty feet from the foot of the tree. It was the sound of a big animal, but nothing was there. Something large and heavy was coming down the trail, toward me.

For several minutes, I could clearly hear it, but not see anything. Finally, I saw it. Coming down the middle of the deer trail was a giant rattlesnake. It was moving slowly, but it was large and heavy enough to make noise on the dry forest floor. It took me a minute to process what I was seeing. It almost did not seem real, and I wanted to get closer. I shimmied down the tree, grabbed my bow, and started to slowly walk toward the deer trail and snake. The snake felt the vibrations of my approach and coiled up under some low branches, rattling while facing me. It was a big snake. I had heard stories about rattlesnake heads being as large as a fist. This one was pretty close, a tad over six feet long, and heavy.

As with anything we are passionate about, we may carry regrets. I have regrets from my sporting life. Part of one's connection to the outdoors is the responsibility to protect it. I regret to this day shooting that snake. I only had my bow and, even at just five yards, the shot placement had to be precise. The snake was coiled on itself with its head lying across the top coil, leaving a pencil eraser-sized spot on the head where the snake would be killed instantly and the skin would not be cut by the arrow's broad head tip. I did not have the skill for such a precise shot. It was just downright lucky.

I returned to camp to skin the incredible snake. Mike Owens, one of my early hunting mentors mentioned earlier in the book, came out to see what I had. There was no admiration in his eyes when he saw the big snake. "I wish people would stop killing the big diamondbacks," he said. He did not say it as a challenge or lecture; he just said it in general, which was far worse. Rattlesnakes, like any animal, have behavioral traits. Some tend to rattle more than others as a warning when approached. Some remain completely silent. The ones who rattle a warning are less dangerous, but tend to be the ones noticed and killed. That particular snake, in that location, was no threat to anyone, and I should have let it go.

As a kid back in Florida, Bill Fuchs could get twenty-five cents for a live water moccasin or up to three dollars for an occasional coral snake. One of Bill's childhood friends, while looking for the more valuable species, was bitten by a Florida coral snake while they were snake hunting one day near their home. He received medical attention, but the bite nearly killed him. The long physical recovery eventually caused his friend to have to drop out of school in the seventh grade.

When he was older, Bill found a great big rattlesnake one day in the Everglades. The giant diamondback was measured at seven feet, four inches long. Bill's good friend Bobby Leach had come back from Vietnam and was working as a bulldozer operator.

Bill had recently left the hospital after the spear fishing accident that blew up his hand and was still covered in bandages. They decided to go snake hunting. Bobby's father owned a construction company in south Florida and was clearing land along the boundary of Everglades National Park. There were big brush piles on the cleared land. Bobby would take a small bulldozer—with Bill hanging on to the hood with his good hand—run it up on the brush piles, and roll the brush over looking for snakes.

"There were always lots of snakes," Bill recalled. "Plenty of rattlesnakes, plenty of moccasins, maybe even an indigo."

Bobby pushed over one pile and Bill yelled from the hood, "Bobby ... Bobby ... stop ... stop!" There was a huge snake.

Bobby yelled back, asking, "How big?"

"It's huge," Bill yelled, adding, "and you're gonna have to help me catch it 'cause I ain't got but one good hand."

Bobby took one look at the giant rattlesnake and said, "Fuchs, I ain't getting off the dozer. You can do what you want. Shoot it ... but I ain't moving."

Bill walked over to a wall in his studio and showed me the picture of his friend Bobby Leach holding that giant rattlesnake, adding, "It's an impressive one."

In North America, with the exception of the reclusive coral snake, which possesses a potent neurotoxin, the more common pit vipers like rattlesnakes, moccasins, and copperheads have hemotoxic venom. Hemotoxin attacks the red-blood cells and causes tissue damage. This deterioration can cause lifelong tissue damage to a human limb. While birding in Costa Rica, I became good friends with a naturalist and avid birder named Carlos. Carlos and I have explored the Osa Pensinsula extensively, looking for various endemic species of birds. One day when I was not with him, Carlos was guiding a group of naturalists up a steep jungle path and reached out for a root to pull himself up. A fer-de-lance, a dangerous pit viper found throughout Central America, was sunning itself on the same root, out of Carlos's sight. As Carlos reached up, he took a direct hit with a full dose of venom on the hand. Carlos was lucky to keep his hand. I have heard stories of locals who lost their legs to fer-de-lance bites, the tissue blackening and falling off their legs, before being amputated. Carlos recovered after agonizing for weeks in the hospital and serious rehab. Years later, we continued to go bird-watching together, but he has never regained full use of his hand.

The cabin in Costa Rica where our family stayed had a small pond out front. The pond was full of tree frogs, giant toads, and various venomous snakes, including one particularly large fer-de-lance. Sue, the kids, and I would walk out each night with headlamps to watch that big viper come down toward the edge of the pond. The snake would extend its triangular head out, hovering right behind, but above, the lineup of frogs at the water's edge. It was an unreal sight. The frogs were facing toward the water, completely unaware of the death hanging right behind them. The snake would reach out and gently taste the back of each frog with its flicking tongue, looking for one without the protective skin toxins so common in Central American frogs. The first frog without skin toxin was toast.

Sporting similar venom as the pit vipers of the Americas, the vipers of Africa include the infamous puff adder. The puff adder is a thick-bodied, slow-moving, temperamental snake, reminiscent of the water moccasin in the US. They have enormous fangs and an incredibly rapid strike. As a defensive measure, the dramatically patterned snake relies on camouflage to avoid detection, which unfortunately results in encounters with those tromping through the bush. As a result, the puff adder is considered Africa's most dangerous snake, and responsible for most serious snakebites in the region. The venom is slower moving and, while deadly, most fatalities are prevented with medical care within twenty-four hours.

The first puff adder I encountered in the bush was heard at first, not seen. My friend and PH, Chap Esterhuizen, who I mentioned in the last chapter, had remarked how his trackers will "hear" snakes, and you will immediately know they have heard a snake from their reaction. Chap's senior tracker, Shaderick, was warily leading us along a low ridge in the Matetsi, downwind of fifty cape buffalo which had winded us an hour before after a gust of back luck. The buffalo were close. Close enough to hear. Shaderick's steps were cautious but deliberate. Chap followed Shaderick and I followed Chap, knowing to step where they step. Suddenly the buffalo were there, twenty paces away and, surrounded by his harem, was our old bull. Chap put up the sticks (the high grass of Africa typically requires shooting off a pod of sticks from a standing position) and I stepped forward. As I placed my rifle on the sticks and adjusted my scope down for the closer than expected encounter, Shaderick hissed a warning. He heard a snake. Chap turned, then I did. Not ten feet away, moving slowly in our direction along a small dried tree branch lying in the rocks and short grass, was a big puff adder.

This was a quandary. We couldn't move, the thick-bodied snake was inching closer, and the old bull we had been chasing for three days was standing twenty yards in front of us. At that moment, he was buffered by cows and offered no shot. However, the crowded herd was constantly adjusting and even the wise old bull could expose a shot opportunity at any moment. We opted to remain focused on the bull. The slight wisp of breeze was in our favor. I turned back to the buffalo and found the bull in my sight. The breeze slowed and—with the exception of random sounds from the herd—it was silent. That's when I heard the snake. The puff adder made a distinct sound as its fat intestine of a body slowly rippled forward along the rocks. I could see it moving on the ground from the corner of my eye as I tried to remain focused on the black mass of buffalo bodies in the scope. That was as pure an "Africa" moment as I have had. The big snake moved closer, the sea of cows never parted and the tension was relieved by another unlucky change of wind direction, which raised every buffalo head in alarm. Fifty tons of buffalo turned and thundered away. I took one last look at the big snake, noticing how beautifully patterned it really was, and slowly followed Shaderick and Chap off the hill.

As noted earlier, Chap's family is from Bulawayo in southwest Zimbabwe. His great uncle had a small plot of land not far from Bulawayo where he raised chickens, sheep and pigs. He had been losing chicks from his coop. One cold morning he found the culprit hiding among the chickens, a heavily-bodied, four-foot snake. He noticed the head, size and pattern of the snake and assumed it was a small python. He picked up the snake, which was lethargic from the cold air, placed it in a sack and took it to the factory where he worked. Chap's great uncle placed the sack on his desk, reached in and looked at the snake. It was beautifully patterned. He realized the snake in a sack could be a perfect opportunity to scare a few fellow employees and asked a couple to "check on some new parts sitting in a sack on his desk." As they got the startle of their life when they went to reach in the sack, Chap's great uncle called a local museum to identify which species of python they had captured. The museum employee took the call and began to ask detailed questions about the shape of the head and skin pattern. While pythons and vipers both have an angular extended head shape, this was not a python. They had captured a huge puff adder. The expert told Chap's great uncle to immediately secure the sack and be very careful. Luckily, the cold morning air made the snake docile and, even with all the handling, it never struck. He put the sack in his truck, drove away from town and released the big snake back into the bush.

Chap enjoys fishing as much as hunting. Years ago, Chap was bass fishing in a small boat near Bulawayo with another PH. As they covered the shoreline with casts, they noticed a small snake swimming in the lake approaching the side of their boat. The foot-long snake was a rhombic night adder, a mildly venomous adder typically found near water sources. Chap and his buddy extended their fishing rods out into the water and tried to flick the snake back toward the shore with the tip of the rods. There were a few missed attempts. Finally his buddy caught the snake on the tip of the rod and gave a quick flick. The snake disappeared. Chap and his buddy looked around for the snake … nothing. A second later, the snake, which had been flicked straight up in the air by the whipping rod tip, landed in their boat. The only thing they had to pick up the dangerous snake was their boga grip hand held fish scale, which they finally managed to grab the snake with, placing it right back in the water where it started from.

Unlike a viper's hemotoxin, neurotoxin of the cobras, mambas, and taipans quickly attacks nerve cells. In the days before anti-venom, mamba bites were known to be deadly within twenty minutes. In Tanzania, Bill and Linda Fuchs were accompanying their client, a hunter from Asheville, North Carolina, on safari. The three of them, along with the PH, Brian Van Blerk, and two native trackers were scouting for animal signs along a dirt road in an open-door Land Rover.

Bill recalls, "The tracker scouts who ride in the back are so keenly aware, it's frightening."

As they were driving along the road, one of the scouts yelled, "Mamba! Mamba coming!"

A large black mamba, about nine feet long, emerged from the grass on the side of the road and crossed right in front of the Rover. The PH, who was driving, could not react before the vehicle rolled onto the back of the snake. The mamba struck at the side of the truck as it was hit. The truck had no doors, offering the fully exposed legs of the PH and hunter behind him. The PH quickly backed the truck off the snake. Miraculously, no one was bitten. Once the vehicle backed away, the angry mamba moved off into the grass, its head towering above the blades.

When Chap was sixteen years old, he had a similar mamba experience while riding a motorbike out in the bush near Bulawayo. His was riding behind a childhood friend, who was on his own motorbike. The friend startled a black mamba, not three feet from the bikes as they passed. As Chap was second in line he saw the angry snake rear up, just missing his bike and leg as they motored past.

Black mamba's can raise their heads up over a third of their body length. That means a ten to twelve foot mamba can rise up over four feet and look at you. That unnerving stare is coupled with aggression, lighting speed and death. I can't imagine a scarier critter to come across in the wild. Rob Lurie's family had a sand business near Harare, the capital of Zimbabwe. One afternoon his father was driving along the sand pits when a huge mamba came after the truck. Luckily the windows were up. His father recalls the mamba striking the outside glass of the truck door window, right at his resting arm. It was a big truck, and the window was a good five feet off the ground.

The Fuchs had another close encounter with a mamba, this time at Paul Jelonek's camp in Zimbabwe. Bill notes, "You never take food back to your tent. Mice follow food … mamba follow mice."

Bill and Linda were having breakfast at camp. Paul came up to join them. As he approached, he told Evileen, the camp maid, that something was crawling around in his tent the night before. He said it was probably a small lizard or frog and asked if she would go check his tent. Evileen didn't particularly want to deal with a frog or lizard but went over to Paul's tent and looked. Her scream shook Paul and the Fuchs to the core. They ran over to find Evileen standing in front of Paul's tent. On the floor inside was a huge black mamba.

"It came right out the front door, progressively and fast," Bill recalled. "They don't play around—they are like a black racer versus a slow moccasin."

The mamba flew out the front door of the tent, right past Bill, Linda, Evileen, and Paul, and went straight up the nearest tree at the edge of camp. Paul grabbed his shotgun and quickly dispatched the big mamba in the tree.

Another time, Bill and his son Jason were on safari hunting eland in Zimbabwe, again with Paul Jelonek. Eland is the largest antelope in the world. They can be five feet at the shoulder and weigh up to two thousand pounds. Eland meat is a delicacy and favorite at hunting camps and local villages. Early one morning, they climbed one of the endless, small, rocky hills, or koppies, that cover the landscape to get a vantage point to glass for eland. Jason was fourteen at the time and started looking around the rocks. "Hey, Dad, I found a snake shed," he said.

Bill replied, "Cool, let's have a look at it. Bring it over."

The PH took one look at the shed and knew exactly what it was. It was a recent shed from a big mamba, probably watching them at that moment. Mambas grow quickly at first, reaching three feet after their first year of life, then six feet after two. A mature mamba can reach twelve or fourteen feet in length, although most are eight to nine feet at maturity.

Paul looked at the shed and said calmly, "Let's get the hell out of here. That's a mamba—a big one."

As they left, Paul continued, "Mamba are territorial as hell. When it warms up, he will come out, lay on the rocks, and look for anything that might disturb him." Today, the Fuchses have a picture of Jason holding that long mamba shed back at their house.

Roy Aylward is a professional hunter and talented wildlife photographer from Zimbabwe. His father was a well-known game warden. Roy grew up living among the animals in the bush. As is everyone in this book, Roy is another great example of a sportsman who understands the balance of hunting and conservation. Roy spent years in Hwange National Park (pronounced "Wange"), the largest park in Zimbabwe. It borders northeastern Botswana, and is home to one of the largest elephant populations in Africa. Roy is modest and soft spoken, so it was with some careful prodding that he agreed to share a mamba story one evening at our camp over a dinner of cape buffalo oxtail soup and buffalo bone marrow with toast.

Roy found a small piece of land near the entrance of Hwange, where he was building a house, or as he jokingly refers a "hut or shack," for his family. The shelter was made of brick with a thatch roof, supporting gum poles and concrete floor. They had no running water. They washed dishes in a small plastic tub, which the resident elephants would try and steal water from every night. Roy laughed "My wife would wake me up each night when the elephants came, upset that the rummaging trunks might break her dishes." He continues, "It was quite rough living in our little hut, but nice to live among the game like that." One day Roy, his wife and two daughters were returning from town. As they pulled up to their new home, still under construction, his eldest daughter said she saw a snake go over the wall into the house. Roy, knowing his daughters were a bit wary of living in the bush, was not convinced she had actually seen a snake. Roy's daughter was adamant however, that she had seen the snake go into the kitchen, which housed shelves with a cloth curtain backing and room for pots and pans. Roy adds, "My wife and daughters refused to leave the car until I went to look for the snake. So I went into the kitchen area, armed with a small stick and pulled back the curtain backdrop from the shelving. And sure as shit, there was a snake, a big one. I could see by the shape of the body and thickness … hmmm. A mamba body is kind of triangular. Up towards the spine it's quite sharp and I knew, chances are, it's a mamba."

Roy yelled for his wife and daughters to go upstairs to the elevated thatch loft, where he felt they would be safe while he dealt with the snake. He continues, "Once my wife and daughters were upstairs, I went into the kitchen and I am trying to get this thing to leave. Because if it leaves, it's got thousands of acres of bush to bugger off into where it came from. So, I'm poking around and the snake is getting pissed off, and the snake keeps moving back into the corner and I keep poking it. Then ... it comes flying out of there. And I say 'flying' because it literally propelled itself across the room, to one of the gum poles, then its body touches the pole and it propels itself two meters to the next pole, and it gets itself up into the attic, the 'safe zone'. It managed to get across a four meter room without touching anything ... so when this thing comes flying out of there, I shit myself, but now I've got three women up on a balcony yelling 'It's coming for you!!'"

Roy's hut had a thatch roof with gum pole cross beams where he stored boards, planks, plywood and a double bed base frame on which he piled boxes of Land Rover spare parts, plenty of places for a mamba to hide. "My wife and kids refused to stay in the shack so I moved them to a camp down the road, where we all spent the night. The next morning, we left the kids at the camp, and my wife and I returned to our hut. I needed her there in case I got bitten," Roy tells me. "As I walked back in the shack, it was the same feeling I get when following a wounded leopard. I had the whole night to think about what I had to face the next day. It's not the most pleasant feeling. I knew the thing should have moved on after being harassed, but it may still be there."

Roy carefully walked into the kitchen and stood up on a forty-four gallon drum to start looking for the snake in the rafters. As he checked each box, he moved it aside. Eventually, all that was left was the double bed base frame. He reached up, moved the bed frame, and could hear the snake moving inside. Roy thought about what to do next. He considered tying a rope to the frame and pulling it out of the house. "I finally decided to call a mate who had a forty-four caliber with snake shot and we just shot the shit out of that bed frame right up in my rafters ... we just stood in the kitchen and shot it to shit ... it never worked as a bed rest again," Roy laughed. "When we pulled the bed frame down and opened it up, the mamba was dead, but you could tell it had been living in there for months. The inside of the frame was covered with snake shit, it had been living among us in the kitchen for months." Later, Roy laid the dead mamba along side his wife for a scale photo (she is evidently quite tall). The snake measured two meters, twenty (over seven feet long).

Back in Queensland, we had plenty of big leeches and spiders, but luckily only a few species of venomous snakes. The red-bellied black snake was probably the one you would most likely encounter. They are quite common in eastern Australia. They have a glossy black back with orange or red sides and belly, and rarely exceed four feet in length. Like cobras, they can flatten their necks to appear larger if threatened. It was highly recommended to wear rubber boots while walking around camp at night in case you stepped on one of these snakes. While the red-bellied black snake's neurotoxin can cause extreme pain and bleeding, it is rarely a fatal bite.

The really scary ones, like the taipan, lived farther east of our school, down in the coastal sugarcane fields. The equally deadly eastern brown snake lived in the farmlands to the west of our school. The taipan in particular is known for its aggressive behavior. Like a mamba, they are incredibly fast and have the unpleasant habit of rearing up while chasing what they see as a threat. There are stories of taipan chasing sugarcane farmers right off their tractors while cutting cane.

I have come close to not making it back a few times in the bush; once or twice in the mountains, a few times in water, and once on a two-track road in northeastern Australia. One of my classmates in Queensland was also fascinated with snakes. The two of us spent much time searching the buttresses of rainforest trees around campus for carpet pythons. One night, our class was returning from a field trip in the Atherton Tablelands, a transition

area between the rainforest and the outback located west of our
school. While not considered true "outback," the Tablelands look
and feel like it. We were driving east, back toward school, on a
two-track dirt road. There is nothing there. No paved roads. No
houses. No civilization for miles. The road has one set of tracks
because so few cars drive it.

As we drove through the black night, our headlights illuminated
a snake ahead in the road. The tail was over halfway across the
road. The head was hidden in the grass and not visible. This made
the snake about eight feet long. We stopped the van, keeping the
snake visible in the headlights. Given the size of the snake, we
assumed it was a carpet python. My buddy and I got ready to jump
out of the van to try and catch it. As I opened the door, one of my
other classmates yelled, "Hey, you should take your flashlight with
you!" That moment saved my life. I grabbed the Maglite, the same
one I used to watch my eight-eyed sleeping partner back in my
cabin, and jumped out wearing field shorts and sneakers.

The two of us approached the snake, about twenty yards in
front of the truck. Our shadows lengthened and softened as we got
farther from the vehicle's headlamps. Even in shadow, the snake's
size was apparent. It was a cold night, which is why the snake
was there to begin with, warming itself on the hardened road. If it
had been warmer, I am sure the snake would have felt us coming
up the road and disappeared into the grass. We figured the snake
would be lethargic in the cool night air.

I offered to go for the head in the grass. My friend positioned
himself to grab the tail. As I bent forward to grab the snake, I
flashed the Maglite across the snake's back. I knew immediately we
had made a terrible mistake. The snake did not have the patterned
markings of a carpet python; it was a muted brown, making it
either a taipan or eastern brown snake, two of the three deadliest
snakes in the world.

If I had tried to grab the head, or if my friend had pulled the snake out by the tail, I would have been bitten on exposed skin. With anti-venom over an hour away, I likely would have died of respiratory failure or cardiac arrest on that two-track dirt road. I was incredibly naive and careless that night. Not to mention, the area we were driving was not remotely conducive, at all, to carpet python. Rushing to grab a snake in the dark, in the Australian bush, has got to be one of the stupidest things one can do. None of my guide friends would have done that.

South America is home to some of the largest snakes in the world. While not venomous, boa, and especially anaconda, achieve enormous proportions. Bill Fuchs recalled one day when he had been fishing in the Amazon. The water was particularly clear. Bill snagged his lure on a palm root near the side of the river and was leaning over the bow to pull it loose. His native guide, affectionately called "Popcorn" by his American friends, suddenly began yelling, "Billy, Billy, no, no!"

Bill pulled his hand back, thinking Popcorn had spotted a wasp nest in one of the overhanging branches. Popcorn yelled, "Look, look!"

Swimming up the river, right in front of Bill, was a fifteen-foot anaconda. Its body was five or six inches wide, not a particularly big anaconda, but large enough to startle Bill and Popcorn. That experience with the fifteen-foot snake made Bill realize just how big the larger anaconda were, the ones that were a foot across.

Bill and Linda Fuchs outfitted guided trips in South America as well as Africa. One year, they had two clients from Tallahassee join them in the Amazon to go fishing for peacock bass. Peacock bass are a voracious predatory sport fish native to South America, although escaped peacock bass are now living in the canals of south Florida. Despite the common name, peacock are not actually bass. They are in the cichlids genus of tropical fish. Like bass fishing, you cast into the structure along the riverbanks. The best peacock fishing occurs during the years when river water levels are low. In these conditions, the river does not flood the jungle, and peacock movement is restricted to the main river channel. In years with high water, the river floods the banks, and the peacock prowl far into the jungle trees, well beyond casting range.

The sides of the river Bill and his clients were fishing were lined with tall, narrow palm trees, which grew out from the banks in various directions. Many of the palm trunks grew out from the riverbank submerged just under the surface of the water, with the crown and fronds emerging well out in the river. These submerged palms were a nuisance for fishermen who would tangle their lures, but they were also a real danger to boats and canoes that would get caught on the hidden trunk in the current.

Bill and his clients were drifting for peacock in separate boats, not far from each other, each with their own native guide. Bill's trusted guide, Carlinos, was running the clients' boat. Carlinos was on the bow, running the trolling motor, while the two fishermen cast along the riverbank. Their outboard, which was hanging off the stern, suddenly got hung up on one of the sunken palms. Carlinos moved to the stern to pull the outboard off what he assumed was a palm trunk. He leaned over the edge and reached his hands down into the water to feel for the skeg, or bottom of the outboard. He could tell the motor was indeed stuck on something big. He continued feeling around with his hands. Carlinos suddenly reeled back and started screaming.

The outboard was not stuck on a palm trunk; it was stuck on the body of a massive snake. Bill heard the commotion and turned his boat to go see what Carlinos was screaming about. By this time, the snake's head appeared in reaction to all the activity farther down its body. As Bill approached, Carlinos was screaming, the two clients were jumping around the boat, and the massive snake was trying to crawl over the stern. Carlinos jumped back on the bow, restarted the trolling motor, and was able to pull forward as the foot-wide anaconda fell back into the water and disappeared.

Bill looked at me and said, "That was a big-ass anaconda, a big female."

As noted earlier with great white sharks, in many animals, the females are larger than the male. Interestingly, the anaconda has the largest female-to-male size difference ratio of all land vertebrates, females being nearly five times larger than males on average.[17]

"Those boys from Tallahassee had had enough; they were ready to go, so they went back to the big boat and started drinking," Bill laughed.

Big female anacondas can weigh five hundred pounds, be over a foot in diameter, and exceed twenty-five feet in length. Bill never saw the biggest snake he came across, but he saw the tracks. The water levels were low that year, revealing long, muddy sandbars along the river's edge. Bill was fishing with Popcorn on one of these sandbars. They came across a giant track in the mud. The track was nearly sixteen inches across, and Bill thought it must have been made by the belly of a large crocodile sliding down into the river.

He looked at Popcorn and said, "Look! Look! Crocodile?"

Popcorn looked at the track, "No, Billy. Look, no feet ... no feet."

There were no crocodile footprints. Popcorn whispered, "Anaconda ... big anaconda."

EPILOGUE

I hope you enjoyed the stories in this book. I enjoyed writing them, but most of all, I enjoyed listening to them being told. The spirit of the guides' stories is in their spoken words, as told in the field, and my written words don't capture that spirit.

There are some guides in this book I may not see again. I treasure the moments I have been allowed to spend with aboriginal people and the Inuit, but I know the chances of our life-paths crossing again is probably remote. On the other hand, I continue to be close friends with most of the guides. Seth and I have many fly fishing adventures ahead of us, including a bowfin trip on the Black River. Steele and I will keep exploring swamps together. Rob, Chap, Jimmy and I will plan many more trips to Africa. I have finally built enough lottery points in Wyoming to draw an elk tag in the Bighorns and should begin planning that hunt with Mark and Valerie Condict in the near future. I hopefully have a few more sheep hunts in me. Mike McCann and I enjoy sharing articles and stories we have each written, and I look forward to sending him a copy of this book to enjoy reading or, worst case, to start a fire with in his trapper's cabin stove in the Wrangells.

My friend Bill Fuchs passed away during the printing of this book. Bill's knowledge and life experiences were a huge inspiration to me as a writer, and also as an outdoorsman. Bill and Linda were always generous with their time, and I treasure the afternoons I spent sitting with Bill in their studio, listening to incredible stories. I know Bill was excited about the book, and he was a fundamental part of it.

As I noted earlier, an entire volume of books could be written about each of these people. Their stories never end because their lives are one long story, and I'll listen in every chance I get. I feel lucky they shared a few stories with me, and that they trusted me to share them with you.

Through their stories, I am reminded of my own connection to the outdoors. Those early years on the small farm in New York, and chasing bluefish up and down the Outer Banks, formed that connection. Time in the field adds perspective, which allows appreciation and, finally, understanding.

I believe our connection to the outdoors, and to those we share it with, can be spiritual in a sense. In the final verse of *A River Runs Through It*, Norman Maclean reveals, "I am haunted by waters."[18] He is speaking from the context of rivers running together, merging all things in life. To me, it speaks to the contrast of our own mortality to timeless places like rivers and mountains.

When I return to those places, I am haunted by the memories of those whom I shared those places with. Not haunted in a bad way. I just feel their presence among the trees or in the sound of the water. They are good memories, and form my eternal connection with everyone in this book. And in that way, the connection is timeless.

BIBLIOGRAPHY

Capstick, Peter Hathaway. *Death in the Long Grass* (New York: St. Martin's Press, 1977). 220.

Capstick. *Death in the Long Grass.* 249.

Census Viewer. "Bettles, Alaska Population: Census 2010 and 200 Interactive Map, Demographics, Statistics, Quick Facts." Bettles, Alaska. http://censusviewer.com/city/AK/Bettles.

Ceurstemont, Sandrine. "Snake sex is every bit as peculiar as you would expect." *BBC Earth.* June 9, 2017. http://www.bbc.com/earth/story/20170608-snake-sex-is-every-bit-as-peculiar-as-you-would-expect.

Descola, Philippe. *In the Society of Nature: A Native Ecology in Amazonia. Vol. 93. Cambridge Studies in Social and Cultural Anthropology.* Trans. Nora Scott (Cambridge: Cambridge University Press, 1996).

Goldstein, Robert J. *Coastal Fishing in the Carolinas: From Surf, Pier, & Jetty* (Winston-Salem: John F. Blair Publishing, 2000).

Grant, Wayne. *Into the Thorn* (Zimbabwe: Mag-Set Publications, 2008).

Gray, T. C. "The Use of d-tubocurarine Chloride in *Anaesthesia*." Anesthesiology 9 (May 1948): 326. https://doi.org/10.1097/00000542-194805000-00026.

Guinness World Records. "Largest spider." Records. 2021. https://www.guinnessworldrecords.com/world-records/largest-spider.

Helmuth, Laura. "Can This Swamp Be Saved?: Bold Everglades-protection strategies may revive the river of grass." *Science News* 155. No. 16 (April 1999): 252. https://doi.org/10.2307/4011388.

Hughes, R. H. and J. S. Hughes. *A Directory of African Wetlands* (Gland, Switzerland, and Cambridge: International Union for Conservation of Nature and Natural Resources; Nairobi: United Nations Environment Programme; Cambridge: World Conservation Monitoring Centre, 1992).

Langenheim, Johnny. "Four places where humans are living in sync with the natural world." *National Geographic.* July 23, 2019. https://www.nationalgeographic.com/environment/article/partner-content-living-in-sync-with-the-natural-world.

Maclean, Norman. *A River Runs Through It* (Chicago: The University of Chicago Press, 1976). 161.

Mitchell, Ed. "Homer Rhode Jr." *Fly Fishing in Salt Waters.* No. 38 (November/December 2011): 44. https://www.edmitchelloutdoors.com/Archives/Homer%20Rhode.pdf.

Mitchell. "Homer Rhode Jr." *Fly Fishing.* 44.

Nolan, Edward J. *Proceedings of the Academy of Natural Sciences of Philadelphia,* 1885 (London: Forgotten Books, 2018).

Rubenstein, Steven Lee. *Circulation, Accumulation, and the Power of Shuar Shrunken Heads.* Vol. 22. No. 3. *Cultural Anthropology* (Hoboken: Wiley, 2007).

Szalay, Jessie. "Giant Huntsman Spider: World's Largest Spider By Leg Span." Animals. Live Science. November 12, 2014. https://www.livescience.com/41428-huntsman-spider.html.

ENDNOTES

1 Robert J. Goldstein, *Coastal Fishing in the Carolinas: From Surf, Pier, & Jetty* (Winston-Salem: John F. Blair Publishing, 2000).
2 "Bettles, Alaska Population: Census 2010 and 200 Interactive Map, Demographics, Statistics, Quick Facts," Bettles, Alaska, Census Viewer, http://censusviewer.com/city/AK/Bettles.
3 Laura Helmuth, "Can This Swamp Be Saved?: Bold Everglades-protection strategies may revive the river of grass," Science News 155, no. 16 (April 1999): 252, https://doi.org/10.2307/4011388.
4 Ed Mitchell, "Homer Rhode Jr.," *Fly Fishing in Salt Waters*, no. 38 (November/December 2011): 44, https://www.edmitchelloutdoors.com/Archives/Homer%20Rhode.pdf.
5 ——, "Homer Rhode Jr.," *Fly Fishing*, 44.
6 Philippe Descola, In the Society of Nature: A Native Ecology in Amazonia, vol. 93, Cambridge Studies in Social and Cultural Anthropology, trans. Nora Scott (Cambridge: Cambridge University Press, 1996).
7 Steven Lee Rubenstein, *Circulation, Accumulation, and the Power of Shuar Shrunken Heads*, vol. 22, no. 3, *Cultural Anthropology* (Hoboken: Wiley, 2007).
8 Edward J. Nolan, *Proceedings of the Academy of Natural Sciences of Philadelphia, 1885* (London: Forgotten Books, 2018).
9 T. C. Gray, "The Use of d-tubocurarine Chloride in Anaesthesia," *Anesthesiology* 9 (May 1948): 326, https://doi.org/10.1097/00000542-194805000-00026.

10 Johnny Langenheim, "Four places where humans are living in sync with the natural world," *National Geographic*, July 23, 2019, https://www.nationalgeographic.com/environment/article/partner-content-living-in-sync-with-the-natural-world.

11 "Largest spider," Records, Guinness World Records, 2021, https://www.guinnessworldrecords.com/world-records/largest-spider.

12 Jessie Szalay, "Giant Huntsman Spider: World's Largest Spider By Leg Span," Animals, Live Science, November 12, 2014, https://www.livescience.com/41428-huntsman-spider.html.

13 Wayne Grant, *Into the Thorn* (Zimbabwe: Mag-Set Publications, 2008).

14 R. H. Hughes and J. S. Hughes, *A Directory of African Wetlands* (Gland, Switzerland, and Cambridge: International Union for Conservation of Nature and Natural Resources; Nairobi: United Nations Environment Programme; Cambridge: World Conservation Monitoring Centre, 1992).

15 Peter Hathaway Capstick, *Death in the Long Grass* (New York: St. Martin's Press, 1977), 220.

16 ——, *Death in the Long Grass*, 249.

17 Sandrine Ceurstemont, "Snake sex is every bit as peculiar as you would expect," *BBC Earth*, June 9, 2017, http://www.bbc.com/earth/story/20170608-snake-sex-is-every-bit-as-peculiar-as-you-would-expect.

18 Norman Maclean, *A River Runs Through It* (Chicago: The University of Chicago Press, 1976), 161.

AUTHOR'S NOTE

This book is a collection of stories from guides, outfitters, professional hunters and trappers I have been fortunate to share a few campfires with, and even more fortunate to call my friends. They have lived and worked in the Wrangell Mountains of Alaska, the Wind River Range of Wyoming, the deep bayou of Louisiana, the Everglades of southern Florida, the savanna and bushveld of Africa and along the rivers of Central and South America. Each one has a life story that could be its own volume of books. This small collection offers just a glimpse, a few of their stories or comments that made me think, smile, or just shake my head in disbelief.